THE CITY GARDENER

BEAUTIFUL GARDENS FOR SMALL SPACES

MEG HERD

Angus&Robertson

An imprint of HarperCollinsPublishers

Angus & Robertson
An imprint of HarperCollins*Publishers*, Australia

First published in Australia in 1995

Copyright © HarperCollins*Publishers*, 1995

HarperCollins*Publishers*
25 Ryde Road, Pymble, Sydney NSW 2073, Australia
31 View Road, Auckland 10, New Zealand
77–85 Fulham Palace Road, London W6 8JB, United Kingdom
Hazelton Lanes, 55 Avenue Road, Suite 2900, Toronto, Ontario M5R 3L2
and 1995 Markham Road, Scarborough, Ontario M1B 5M8, Canada
10 East 53rd Street, New York NY 10032, USA

National Library of Australia Cataloguing-in-Publication data:
Herd, Meg.
The city gardener: beautiful gardens for small spaces.
    Includes index.
    ISBN 0 207 18902 1.
    1.Balcony gardening. 2.Patio gardening. 3.Roof gardening. 4.Courtyard gardens. I.Title.
    635.9671

Printed in Hong Kong
Cover photograph by Lorna Rose
Internal photographs copyright © Lorna Rose, with the exception of the following:
p.20 (top), p.32 (bottom), p.34 (top), p.35 (top).
Illustrations by Justin Sayers
Design by Kerry Klinner

9 8 7 6 5 4 3 2 1
95 96 97 98 99

Contents

Introduction

Having a small garden — as opposed to having a large, rambling one — has many advantages.

With the busy lifestyle and frenetic pace dictated by modern life, many a gardener has little time left to devote to managing and maintaining a substantial space. A small area can be designed attractively and economically, and kept looking beautiful, without its owner being overwhelmed by never getting on top of it and feeling a slave to the garden.

The smallest pocket-handkerchief garden, courtyard or balcony can be moulded into a green haven: a place for adults to relax and entertain, or a place for children to play and potter. A small garden can become a place for enthusiastic cooks to grow their own produce, or for the frazzled just to sit and smell the flowers.

Smaller spaces do, however, place certain restrictions upon the design of the garden, and a few landscape principles should be adhered to in order to create a peaceful and harmonious outdoor area.

The planting of a small plot also requires the gardener to exercise discipline with plant selection — every favourite or desired plant cannot be accommodated in a small garden as it could in a larger one — this restraint inevitably results in a better designed and thought-out landscape.

Design principles
for small-scale gardens

PREVIOUS PAGE:
A welcoming shady spot
in the summer heat:
stepping stones lead to a
birdbath and a cool stone
bench, in the dappled
shade of a small garden.

BELOW: *When planning a*
small garden, remember
that simple, uncluttered
and symmetrical designs
will go a long way to
creating a calm and
relaxing environment.

❧ CLEAN AND UNIFIED DESIGN

If the garden is being started from scratch or is being remodelled, keep in mind when setting out beds, planting areas and hard-landscaping features (such as paving, paths or decks), that simplicity will lead to good design.

The smaller the area, the more important it is to plan the overall space symmetrically, incorporating clean geometric lines, without sweeping curves, fussy meandering paths and dotty beds. Keeping the basic design lines uncluttered will also work well for small cottage-style gardens, when an abundant effect is achieved by exuberant planting within a well-defined basic structure.

It is imperative that the planting scheme is simple and cohesive — resist the temptation to incorporate every possible garden style or plant into a scheme. This will eliminate a hotchpotch effect, and will ensure the development of a restful and stylish space in which to garden, entertain and relax.

❧ PROPORTION AND SCALE

Consider the ultimate size of the trees and shrubs to be planted. It is important that the landscaping treatment is in scale with the size of the garden and the surrounding space and buildings.

It is a considerable advantage to be able to incorporate a small to medium tree into any garden. A tree takes up less ground space than a shrub — when mature, a tree's canopy occupies aerial space, but its trunk does not take up much garden area. Whether the area under consideration is a courtyard garden or only a minute backyard, a tree whose size is in proportion to the area will add needed dimension and act as a focal point.

All space is precious in a tiny garden, and each plant chosen must 'earn its keep', so the tree selected should have as much year-round appeal as possible. Avoid species with leaves of indifferent quality: favour those with foliage that is interesting throughout all seasons. The addition of decorative flowers and/or fruits is an added bonus.

Species with an attractive trunk and bark may be given preference, as it is precisely these features that will be at eye level when at maturity.

Moderately high-branching species of trees are much more functional than vase-shaped ones, as they allow for people to move around underneath them and utilise the existing space as well as providing shelter and shade. The types of trees which are notably susceptible to disfiguring pests and diseases should be eliminated.

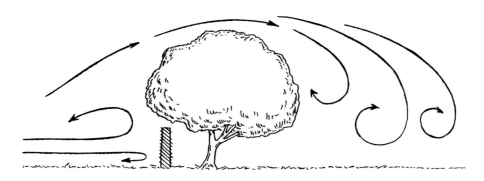

LEFT: *This illustration demonstrates the wind flow around different windbreaks. If you do use a solid windbreak such as a wall, make sure it is on the outside of your garden and does not turn the wind in a direction that may affect another part of the garden.*

Finally, restrict the plants you choose for your garden to those of small to medium habit that will not eventually overpower their allotted space, and do not select those with a reputaion for interfering with paving, paths or drains.

🌱 MICROCLIMATE

A microclimate is a small climate within the garden. It is affected by the immediate surroundings, and varies from that of the general area. Such variation may result from, for example, a courtyard with heat-reflecting walls, or a wind channel, or the vegetation itself. All such factors will influence the plants grown in the microclimate.

It is possible to take advantage of a favourable microclimate and modify an unfavourable one.

TEMPERATURE

Dark colours (which absorb the heat) become much hotter than light ones (which reflect it). Therefore, the colour of a deck, patio or court-yard will affect the plants on and around it. For example, a potted plant, even if it is sun-tolerant, may have its fine feeding roots burned if it stands on a dark surface on a hot day without any protection.

A warm microclimate can be created in a cool region by the building of white-painted brick walls around a sheltered courtyard. The walls can be used to espalier fruit trees, such as apricots and peaches, which would not otherwise ripen their fruits.

WIND

Wind can create microclimates detrimental to all but the hardiest plants. Wind cannot be stopped, but its force can be modified.

A combination of open and solid material is required to modify the wind's velocity and allow the gusts to pass through — solid walls and fences merely channel the wind in a different direction, and may even increase its force.

A staggered row of sturdy trees and shrubs would be effective as a windbreak, as screens of living plants have the required ratio of open to solid material.

If there is a wind tunnel between the house and fence, erect a small lattice screen at the entrance to the passage to modify the wind's force.

ABOVE AND BELOW:

*With a little imagination
even the smallest space
can become a green
haven in which to relax
and entertain.*

VEGETATION

The vegetation itself can affect the microclimate. The microclimate beneath a canopy of trees and shrubs will be more temperate than the surrounding garden. Mulching the soil beneath plants will help to keep soil temperatures more even.

🌿 PRIVACY AND SCREENING

In small gardens in densely populated areas, privacy and screening assume paramount importance for owners who wish to create an inner sanctum away from neighbours and the hustle and bustle of street traffic and city noise.

Treatments that may be considered include lattice work covered with neat vines, hedges, fences camouflaged with espaliered

LEFT: *Unless your garden is absolutely tiny, it should be possible to grow a single specimen tree of small to medium size. Japanese Maples (for example, Acer palmatum 'Dissectum atropurpureum') provide a beautiful autumn display.*

shrubs, and pergolas dripping with leafy climbers.

In more sizeable spaces pleaching (clipping trees so their canopies form an elevated-hedge effect) is perfect for a privacy screen at a height.

The norm, unfortunately, is a garden boxed in with a paling fence. With a little forethought and imagination, a paling fence can be turned into an attractive feature. The fence can be painted (green timber finish is an unobtrusive and attractive colour in the garden) and lattice bolted or nailed on top of it. This in itself provides an ornamental finish, but delicate climbers can also be added.

There are many delicate climbers suitable for lattice, including *Gelsemium sempervirens* (Carolina Jasmine), with fragrant yellow, funnel-shaped flowers, *Solanum jasminoides* (White Potato Vine) and *Sollya heterophylla* (Blue-bell Creeper).

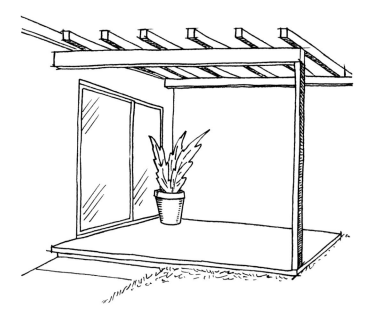

Vigorous climbers such as *Wisteria sinensis* (Chinese Wisteria), *Lonicera* species (Honeysuckle) and *Jasminum* species (Jasmine) become too intrusive and require much stronger support than lattice.

A latticed fence in a sunny area also provides the perfect opportunity to grow annual sweet peas or climbing or runner beans, if the area is to be a kitchen garden.

PERGOLAS

Pergolas can provide much-needed privacy in gardens overlooked by taller buildings. They may also be partially screened at the sides using slats or lattice. Many themes and variations can be adopted to suit the particular situation and special needs of the site.

Pergolas can be fixed to one or two walls of the house, or they can be free standing. They can be quite easily built over an already existing patio or deck.

Apart from providing privacy, pergolas create an outdoor living area that is a link between the house and the garden. Deciduous vines can be grown on them, to give shade in summer and sunlight in winter when it is most needed.

USING VERTICAL SPACE

In very small gardens, where space is at a premium, it is a good idea to incorporate plants that will occupy vertical space. This can be achieved by using techniques such as espalier, or by planting climbers that will clamber over a pergola and occupy aerial space.

COMPOST BINS

Making compost is an inexpensive and efficient way of continuously improving and nourishing garden soil. Material that can be composted includes: plant and vegetable refuse, seaweed, straw, blood and bone, and animal manure.

For very small city gardens, a compost bin would be more appropriate than a compost heap. Not only would there be insufficient space for a compost heap, but it would be unsightly. (An ideal compost heap would be 2 m sq/6 ft sq and 1 m/3 ft high, too large for a small garden.)

Compost bins are available through garden centres, supermarkets and local councils. They are usually made of a black plastic material and are quite unobtrusive if tucked away in a corner of the garden; however, further disguise can be achieved by screening them off with timber lattice.

THE TECHNIQUE OF ESPALIER

An espalier is a framework (either a solid wall or open fence structure) upon which ornamental or fruit trees and shrubs are trained to grow in a flat plane. Espalier may also refer to the particular plant so trained.

The espalier treatment provides a decorative and often quite symmetrical, formal effect. A firm foundation, such as wires strung along a house wall or fence, must be given against which the plant is to grow. Pot cultivation of espaliers is possible if the pot is large enough for the root system.

Espalier can achieved by stringing wires at 30 cm (1 ft) intervals between two uprights. Place the plant centrally against this support and pinch its top so that it will branch laterally. Cut out all growth, except two strong laterals (or more, if the pattern you are looking for requires it). Then tape the laterals securely at intervals of 15 cm (6 in.) along the bottom wire. The aim is to produce a symmetrical tree. As shoots appear, two more are chosen to grow on the next wire and so on. Tying leaders firmly onto lengths of cane or dowel, and then securing them to the wires, is a common method of training.

It can be a time-consuming form of gardening, as constant watch must be kept over plant growth. Limbs have to be pruned before they become hardwood, and growth should not be trimmed right to the trunk. A short stump could develop fruiting spurs for the next season.

Of the many trees and shrubs which have been tried for espalier work, fruiting and flowering fruit trees, *Camellia sasanqua*, *Cotoneaster*, *Chaenomeles* (Flowering Quince) and *Escallonia* is recommended.

OPPOSITE: *Pergolas are the perfect way to both extend your living area and to add to or enhance your garden area.*

BELOW: *There are many ways of creating an espalier pattern depending on where you pinch out the new growth and how many laterals you leave to train. This illustration demonstrates diagonal, horizontal and slightly angled growth.*

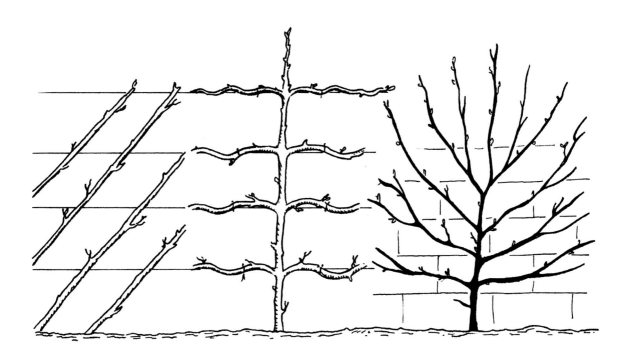

CLIMBING PLANTS

Vines can be used to great effect in small gardens, as they occupy very little ground space. They can be used to outline a special feature, such as an arch, or to hide an ugly building or view; they can provide rapid shade and create privacy. Vines should, however, be used with care in small gardens: avoid rampant climbers, and choose well-behaved and more easily controlled types.

For autumn colour, both Boston Ivy (*Parthenocissus tricuspidata*) and Ornamental Grape (*Vitis vinifera* 'Alicante Bouchet') are spectacular.

There is an enormous number of deciduous and evergreen Asian and European *Clematis*, and they are considered among the most beautiful of all climbing plants. *Clematis* species perform better in cooler climates and prefer a moist, deep, loamy soil with plenty of organic matter.

Passiflora edulis (Passionfruit) is a well-known evergreen climber, and its delicious fruit make it a sensible addition to any garden, especially a a kitchen garden. Two highly ornamental, flowered species can be grown in warm climates: the scarlet flowered *P. manicata* and the ice-blue

ABOVE (TOP AND BOTTOM): *Hard paving is far more practical for small spaces than lawn, whether for a courtyard or a pathway.*

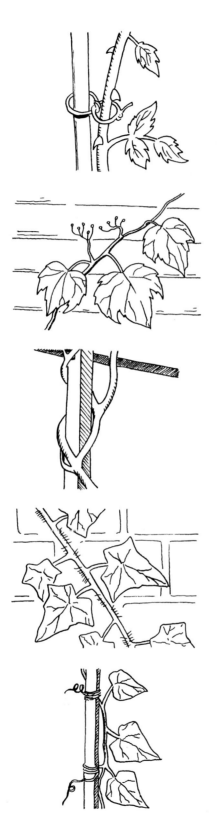

RIGHT: *Climbers occupy vertical and aerial space, and are therefore ideal for the small garden or courtyard. They can be trained on pergolas, arches, trellises, lattices or on walls. Depending on the species, they progress by rambling, with adhesive pads, by twining, with suckers or with tendrils.*

flowered *P. caerulea*. Both grow quickly and are suitable for light trellises, lattice work or pergolas.

Blue-bell Creeper (*Sollya heterophylla*) is a delicate twiner, easily trained for fan-shaped supports against a wall. It has small green leaves, cane-like stems, and an abundance of star-shaped bright blue flowers.

Purple Wreath (*Petrea volubilis*) is a slender twiner, very suitable for archways or lattice. It has large, heart-shaped leaves and sprays of star-like, lilac and purple blossoms.

❧ GROUNDCOVER FOR SMALL AREAS

Although a small lawn is a possibility in limited spaces, there are more practical solutions to covering surface areas. These include paving with 'hard' landscaping materials and using carpeting plants.

PAVING

Bricks or paving stones make excellent pathways or permanent surfaces for outdoor entertainment or wear and tear areas. There is a vast range of colours and a wide range of textures to choose from depening on their use.

Bricks are best laid on a thick bed of sand. In areas that will be subjected to traffic, a dry mortar can be swept into the cracks after the bricks have been laid, and then watered with a fine mist spray. In a few days the bricks are set firm but still look natural.

Tiles are especially impressive when the adjacent indoor area is floored with the same tiles. The effect is particularly spacious, and an integrated effect from indoors to outdoors is created. You might consider quarry tiles, which come in a wide range of colours and textures, and are durable and trouble-free.

Sandstone is another ground-cover that is useful in small gardens. It is available in a smooth (sawn sandstone) or uneven (split) finish, and blends well with the garden. Sandstone can be laid flat on the ground, with spaces left for carpeting plants or herbs.

When laying down hard-surface areas, consider an edging to separate beds from paths. An edging creates a neat and professional look. Examples include low plants such as *Buxus* (Box), bricks set at an angle, or Victorian-style flower-bed edgings in rope or scallop shapes.

CARPETING PLANTS

Carpeting plants can be used for great effect in non-traffic areas. They can also be planted in amongst paved areas to give a softening effect to an otherwise harsh look.

Carpeting plants form a thick mat over the soil and grow no more than 20 cm (8 in.) tall. Some have flowers, others have aromatic leaves; some set down roots as they spread, others sprawl their stems over the ground. All play an important part in any garden and require far less attention than grass; they also discourage the growth of weeds and are an attractive covering for unsightly or bare areas.

Once established, these plants require little of your time in maintenance. A pair of secateurs or

shears, or even the kitchen snips, can trim them in a few minutes. They need watering regularly in summer and occasionally in winter if it is dry, as well as a sprinkling of liquid fertiliser in early spring.

For sunny positions, *Cerastium tomentosum* (Snow in Summer) is perfect. It is a magnificent evergreen groundcover with silvery leaves, and a thick sprinkling of white flowers in summer. Also ideal for sunny spots are *Convolvulus mauritanicus* (Ground Morning Glory), with masses of purple flowers from spring to autumn, and *Campanula portenschlagiana* (Bellflower), with pale blue flowers in spring.

There are several herbs that make useful groundcovers. *Anthemis* (Chamomile) and *Thymus* species (thyme) have aromatic leaves, and enjoy being walked on.

Phyla nodiflora (Lippia) is a rapid-growing groundcover with small leaves and tiny purplish-white flowers. It tolerates heat and drought and light traffic, and grows where many other plants cannot survive.

For semi-shade areas *Dichondra repans* is unbeatable. It is neatly foliaged, readily forms a mat and will thrive in most places. *Heterocentron elegans* (Spanish Shawl) is attractive and useful for binding soil and trails well over rocks or stonework.

For shade or filtered sun areas, clumps of *Viola odorata* (Sweet Violets) are beautiful. The large heart-shaped leaves are present all year, and purple flowers appear in early spring. *Viola hederacea* (Native Violet) will grow happily in the shade whilst producing a little purple and white flower.

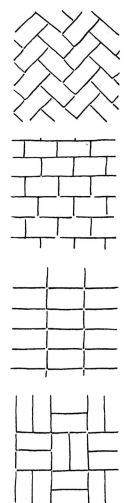

ABOVE: *Paving bricks are not only available in many different patterns and textures, but can be laid in different designs.*

RIGHT: *A plain brick wall can be softened and made attractive with the addition of lattice and a climbing plant.*

FAR RIGHT: *Old bricks, cleaned of mortar and laid in a herringbone pattern, make an excellent groundcovering.*

BELOW: Anthemis (Chamomile) is a useful carpeting plant — it enjoys being walked on.

Specialised small gardens

EASY-CARE GARDENING

• Avoid planting trees that drop their leaves. Although deciduous trees drop their leaves, they do so only for a short period; the eucalypts, however, shed their leaves for months.

• Choose easy-care trees and shrubs, such as: *Camellia sasanqua*, *Gordonia axillaris*, *Lagerstroemia* (Crepe Myrtle), plain or variegated forms of *Elaeagnus pungens*, *Murraya paniculata* (Orange Jessamine), *Abelia grandiflora*, *Coprosma repens* (Looking-glass Plant), and *Chaenomeles* (Flowering Quince).

• Choose plants that are pruned by picking the flowers, such as *Dendranthema frutescens* (Marguerite Daisy), *Dendranthema maxima* (Shasta Daisy), and *Felicia amelloides* (Blue Daisy).

• Choose hardy perennials, such as *Agapanthus*, *Clivia*, *Kniphofia* and *Gazania*.

• Eliminate lawns; pave outdoor living areas and plant groundcovers where necessary.

• Mulch your garden to reduce the need for constant weeding and watering.

• Install a permanent watering system.

• Avoid pot plants and vegetable gardens, as they are labour intensive.

• Do not plant trees and shrubs that need pruning and lopping continuously.

• Avoid planting hedges, especially the fast-growing types that need clipping weekly during the spring and summer growing periods.

• Avoid too many annuals.

• Avoid plants that are subject to pests and diseases.

• Avoid plants that demand regular attention.

Apart from gardens the size of pocket-handkerchiefs, found in the front or backyard of most city terraces or semi-detached buildings, there are patios, courtyards, decks and balconies — unique types of small gardens that call for extra planning and specialised treatment.

❧ PATIO

A patio is an area, usually paved, adjoining a house and open to the sky. It is especially useful in regions where the climate allows outdoor entertaining and protection from sun or wind is needed.

If seclusion is all-important, provide an enclosure by screening part of the patio garden. A screen can be made with a trellis or lattice and a climber such as *Vitis vinifera* 'Alicante Bouchet' (Ornamental Grape) for shade in summer and a beautiful autumn display. Flowering vines can be used in the same way with dramatic effect.

A low brick wall, a hedge, or a row of potted shrubs also provides privacy. If a coping or low wall surrounds the patio, you can plant annuals in garden beds or planter boxes around the perimeter.

The patio is the place where pots and tubs are particularly effective, and containers should harmonise with the house and the paving material.

Hardy and colourful plants for pots and tubs include *Pelargonium* species (Geranium) and *Tropaeolum majus* (Nasturtium).

Choice of shrubs for the patio will vary according to the aspect and

the climate, but plants with perfumed leaves or flowers or those with dramatic flowers or foliage are obvious choices. It is also important to select some evergreen shrubs to keep the area looking furnished throughout the winter months.

❧ COURTYARD

A courtyard is a space enclosed by walls next to or within a house, and provides privacy and shelter. It can be constructed on even the smallest area of land, but it should be architecturally compatible with the adjoining house.

In inner metropolitan areas the courtyard may represent the total garden; or, if space allows, the courtyard may form only part of the garden, being a specialised feature set apart from the rest.

A number of long-life materials are available from which to build the walls, such as natural sandstone, slate, granite, bricks, fibreglass, transparent PVC, sanded glass, palings, tongue and groove, and rounded posts and rails. Flooring can be floorboards (spaced, to allow for run-off), cement squares, tiles, rock,

LEFT: *There can be as many different types of courtyards as there are houses. A courtyard can be any size you want and made from any type of materials you desire.*

BELOW: *Potted shrubs placed in a row on the edge of an open patio can provide privacy and protection from wind.*

PAGE 17: *A wrought-iron table and chairs is a pretty focal point in this lush and private arbour.*

RIGHT: *Prunus sub-hirtella 'Pendula' (Weeping Cherry), can be grown outdoors in pots; after their spring blossoms they can be put into the background until next spring. When in blossom they deserve to be in a focal position.*

BELOW: *This pretty courtyard features an old cast-iron bath filled with an abundance of flowering plants. Although* Campanula medium *(Canterbury Bell) is a biennial, it is grown as an annual in warm climates; flowering from spring to early summer.*

cross-cut sections of logs, tan bark, river pebbles or gravel. When you are choosing, take care to harmonise with the house and consider whether you plan to grow deciduous creepers or vines up the walls or overhead —

autumn leaves can be a nuisance to sweep from some surfaces.

Most courtyards do not have roofs; if shade is required, a courtyard can be roofed with open rafters or slats to support creepers,

they begin looking fussy and cramped if there are too many, so take care — it might be better to subtract rather than add.

If the courtyard is large enough, it may be possible to grow a single specimen tree. Choose a small to medium deciduous tree, such as *Ulmus glabra* 'Lutescens' (Golden Elm) or a small *Acer palmatum* (Japanese Maple), which colours beautifully in autumn and allows winter sun to enter the courtyard.

LEFT: *The side gate of an inner-city cottage leads to a tiny but private oasis of garden.*

BELOW: *No neighbours can see over the walls of this small garden, in which there is an abundance of plant life: azaleas, clivia, aucuba and leopard plant.*

vines and hanging baskets. A fibreglass roof will provide shelter from the wind and will allow sunlight to enter.

Tender plants are happier in a sheltered courtyard than in an open one. Pot plants should be moved and turned regularly so that pests can be detected and growth can be evened out all around the plant.

Troughs and hanging baskets will increase the planting area, and large urns can look very attractive with spillover specimens or small herbaceous climbers. Non-rampant climbers or espaliered fruit trees can be grown against the walls.

While garden ornaments can provide interest in small courtyards,

🌿 Deck

A deck consists of an enclosed or elevated platform or verandah; it is usually made of wood, and should be designed to take advantage of sunshine and breezes.

A good location for a deck is generally on the side of the house where the longest hours of sunshine are received. If the summer sun is fierce, it might be necessary to add a pergola or verandah extension.

A deck that faces the rising sun will be warm in the mornings and cool in the afternoons. One that receives sun in the afternoon might make a successful evening entertainment area. A deck that turns around a shaded corner of the house will enable you to move if the sun gets too hot.

There are other considerations in the placing of your deck, such as privacy (a tall house might overlook your proposed deck) or a view.

A deck is constantly exposed to rain and sun, so choose a timber that will resist warping and rotting. Hardwoods are a popular choice for decks, but even they require some protection against insects, weather and foot traffic. Surface timbers are best protected by stain-type finishes, which have a satin finish and retain the natural look of raw timber. Paint is less able to withstand the combination of traffic and exposure.

Shrubs suitable for growing in containers on decks range from those that enjoy full sun to those happy in the shade. For full sun and positions receiving reflected heat from walls, *Hibiscus rosa-sinensis* (Hibiscus) and *Nerium oleander* (Oleander) are ideal. *Bougainvillea* is also suitable, either as a bush or a climber.

Where there is lots of sunshine but not so much heat, some of the Hawthorns, particularly *Raphiolepis umbellata* and *R. indica*, make attractive and hardy bushes. *Strobilanthes anisophyllus* (Goldfussia), with bronze-purple leaves, and *Fuchsia triphylla* 'Gartenmeister Bonstedt', with vermilion flowers, are also suitable for sunny spots, but they need protection from heat and wind. Many of the conifers are also suitable for containers on a deck.

Azaleas, fuchsias and *Daphne odora* take kindly to containers in the shade. The various *Buxus* species (Box), green or variegated, will also thrive. Amongst the hardy perennials, *Agapanthus* and *Clivia* will perform handsomely in containers on decks.

For a seaside aspect, *Metrosideros excelsa* (New Zealand Christmas Tree) and *Coprosma repens* (Looking-glass Plant) are unaffected by salty winds and are ideal for these areas.

🌿 Balcony

A balcony is a raised, railed platform projecting from the walls of a building. A garden on a balcony can do much towards helping to blend a building with its surroundings, and it may be the only type of garden available to a flat-dweller.

Your choice of plants will be influenced by climatic factors (sunlight, rain and wind), and by the size and shape of your balcony and its intended purpose.

If you are builing a balcony onto an existing structure, consider the sun's aspect in the siting of your balcony. You might wish to position it where it will receive the longest hours of sunshine, or the afternoon sun (which may be very hot in summer), or the morning sun (in which case, the balcony will be warm in the mornings and cool in the afternoons), or plenty of light but no direct sun. Of course, the amount of sunlight on your balcony will also be affected by the shadows of taller buildings.

Other factors to be taken into account include whether your balcony is sheltered from rain or wind by another balcony above or next to it, or whether it is exposed to the elements.

To make the best use of a small space, you might attach planters to the outside of the balcony railings. Hanging baskets can be suspended from wall brackets. Perhaps you could grow climbers around the windows and doors of the balcony to create the impression of overall greenery. If the balcony is intended as an area for entertaining, you'll want to add a table and chairs.

To avoid puddles on your balcony and irritating your downstairs neighbours with drips from pots and hanging baskets, you'll have to do something about drainage. Saucers are an obvious solution, but you could also consider growing plants in individual pots and placing these pots together in a large trough.

A massed planting of one species can be used to create a special effect of colour or greenery, or certain specimens may be chosen for their individual interest and planted to complement each other. As in any garden, it should be remembered that variation in the height, width and shape of the plants, the type of foliage, and the time of flowering all add interest.

For a balcony in a hot or sunny position, *Gazania*, *Mesembryanthemum* and *Osteospermum* are suitable. For a sunny position, you could choose from *Petunia*, *Tagetes*, *Matthiola* (Marigold), dwarf *Antirrhinum*, *Nemesia*, *Lobelia*, *Verbena*, *Dianthus*, *Primula*, *Cheiranthus*, *Viola*, *Pelargonium*, *Tropaeolum*, *Phlox*, *Zinnia*, *Lobularia*, *Gomphrena* and dwarf *Chrysanthemum*, all of which will provide a brilliant display of colour.

For a balcony that does not receive much sun, consider *Impatiens balsamina*, *Senecio* × *hybridus*, *Campanula*, *Primula* × *polyantha*, *Viola odorata* (Sweet Violet), *Myosotis*, *Clivia* and *Begonia*. For spring colour, the following bulbs are excellent and grow easily: *Narcissus* (Daffodil), *Hyacinthus*, *Freesia* and *Endymion* (Bluebell).

ABOVE: *Having a deck is the perfect way to take advantage of a position that provides you with warming sunshine in the winter and cooling breezes in the summer. Make sure you choose plants that can also take advantage of these conditions.*

Azaleas and camellias will flourish if they receive some morning sun but care must be taken so that they are never allowed to dry out. The dwarf Kurume azaleas are particularly appealing. Fuchsias and pendulous begonias are ideal for hanging baskets on a balcony that receives the morning sun.

For a Japanese-style balcony garden, grow small-leafed bamboo, well-trained weeping cherries or a Japanese Maple, a bonsai or two and some Kurume azaleas.

A Mediterranean-style garden can be quite easily established with colourful plants in terracotta pots, baskets of petunias and geraniums, and tubs of citrus trees, small figs and vines.

Balcony gardeners may wish to devote some space to raising vegetables and herbs. Capsicums, eggplants and tiny tomatoes will thrive in a sunny position; a small crop of mignonette lettuces will be ready to eat within 6 weeks. Climbing runner beans are also suitable if lattice, or similar support, is provided. Strawberries take up little space and look decorative grown in tall strawberry pots or tubs.

Citrus trees can be grown in tubs. Their glossy leaves provide interest even when their flowers and fruit are absent. Cumquats are ideal, and mandarins and 'Valencia' oranges are all easily kept to attractive shapes. For a good citrus crop, water regularly and feed two or three times a year with a general fertiliser.

Remember not to overload a balcony; large pots filled with moist soil can be very heavy.

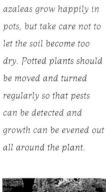

BELOW: Camellias and azaleas grow happily in pots, but take care not to let the soil become too dry. Potted plants should be moved and turned regularly so that pests can be detected and growth can be evened out all around the plant.

Creating stylish
small gardens

❧ THE PETITE FORMAL GARDEN

Simplicity is the key to landscaping formal gardens; clean, strong symmetrical lines provide the basic garden structure, combined with restraint in planting.

A formal treatment is well-suited to the gardens of compact terraces and city cottages: they are of a regular shape, sometimes already bounded by walls or high fences, and therefore easily adapted to symmetrical design. The constant maintenance required to preserve good order in a formal garden (hedges regularly clipped, lawns constantly mown, and paths and beds immaculately tended) means that a formal treatment is a more viable option on the small scale.

The history of formal gardens is considerable, beginning with the formal gardens of the Italian Renaissance and included such features as mazes, knotted flower-beds, shaped hedges, ponds, statuary, paths and garden beds — all laid out in perfect symmetry, order and proportion.

Formal design is emerging as the greatly favoured style of the 1990s. Today it is possible to design and create a formal garden by using well-planned paths, terraces and planting patterns, and by growing species — especially exotic ones — for dramatic effect.

Arches, fountains, espaliers and topiary are all possible components. Exotic stone flagging or concrete is favoured for a formal effect; lawns should be quite level, and the size, shape and colour of flowering plants should be harmonious and ordered.

Hedges are an important feature of the formal tradition. When considering hedges for diminutive gardens choose from those species that are slow growing and will remain in bounds, preferably with a smallish leaf. *Buxus sempervirens* ('Common Box) is a much-used plant for formal hedging. With constant clipping it can be kept as a low border; it will grow taller in old age.

Lonicera nitida (Box-leaved Honeysuckle) is a small shrub, not a vine like its relatives, and is an excellent alternative to a box hedge. The leaves are small, glossy green, lightening to gold-green when planted in full sun.

Lavender makes a beautiful and aromatic hedge border, and is available in several species. It can be pruned to shape by cutting flower spikes for posies or by removing deadheads. Renew lavender plants

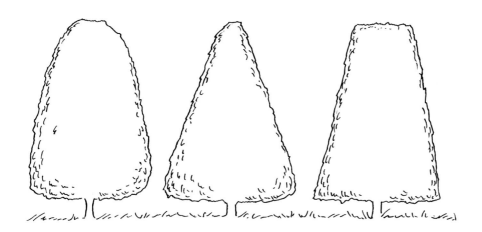

after 4 or 5 years by taking cuttings with a heel in early spring.

Somewhat taller in habit, but capable of being kept to 1 m (3 ft) by clipping, are *Coleonema pulchrum* (Diosma), *Abelia*, *Choisya ternata* (Mexican Orange Blossom) and *Viburnum tinus* (Viburnum).

A successful hedging plant will have the following characteristics: it will thrive under conditions of close planting; it is ornamental for a large part of the year; it is long lived; it is hardy, that is, not prone to disfiguring pests or diseases; it has deep roots, to resist any wind damage; and it appreciates cutting and clipping.

When planting the garden, ensure you choose plants that are elegant and understated. In this way you will complement the formal style rather than dominating it and obscuring its basic structure. Species with a neat habit should be preferred over those which sprawl, and great restraint should be exercised with colour choice and coordination.

When a limited palette is demanded, perfume rather than colour can become a highlight of a garden.

Gardenia species and cultivars (Gardenia) have thick, creamy white, waxy flowers, and a strong perfume. With dense, shiny,

PREPARING A BED

When designing a new garden, it will pay dividends to put effort into the initial bed preparation. This is especially important with the planting of trees and shrubs — they are usually long lived, and once placed it is difficult to move them or to change the soil environment around them.

Bed preparation includes digging, removing stones and weeds and tough roots, and enriching the soil. Take care not to dig deeper than the topsoil, as digging deeply may destroy the soil structure and impair the fertility of the topsoil.

around the 1 m (3 ft) mark. Dark green leaves contrast beautifully with the deep pink buds opening to pale pink, fragrant flowers in winter and spring. *D. o.* 'Alba' has white flowers with a rather sharper perfume, and *D. o.* 'Variegata' has leaves margined with cream.

Philadelphus species (Mock Orange) are elegant shrubs with fragrant flowers. In early summer the long branches arch with their load of single or double white flowers with distinctive yellow stamens. The popular hybrid 'Virginal' grows to 3 m (10 ft). *P. microphyllus* (Small-leafed Mock Orange), growing to 1 m (3 ft), is an excellent alternative where a more compact plant is needed.

Michelia figo (Port Wine Magnolia) has the perfect growing habit for the formal-style garden. Even though its small, wine-red flowers are undistinguished they are very fragrant.

ABOVE: *Cumquat, balsam and a clipped box add formal elegance to a front entrance.*

RIGHT: *Potted topiary, such as this* Buxus sempervirens *(Common Box) in a two-handled urn, is ideal for the formal garden.*

evergreen foliage, and ultimately reaching 2 m (6 ft) high and wide, these shrubs are a perfect choice for a small formal garden. *Gardenia augusta* 'Radicans' is a low-growing, spreading shrub, 30–45 cm (1–1½ ft) in height with smaller leaves and flowers; this is the most suitable species for really tight spaces, pot culture, low borders or rockeries.

Daphne odora can reach 2 m (6 ft) high and wide, but is generally seen

Other plants that are delightfully fragrant and suit the formal style include *Brunfelsia bonodora* (Yesterday-Today-Tomorrow), *Choisya ternata* (Mexican Orange Blossom), *Murraya paniculata* (Orange Jessamine) and *Rondeletia odorata*.

Topiary and 'standard' plants are an integral part of the formal garden; none more beautiful than the standard rose, which takes up very little ground space — due to the pole-trunk and lollipop-crown effect — and is therefore most suitable for gardens small in scale. Many hybrids are available, and choices should be made after consulting nursery catalogues or visiting specialist rose nurseries. However, a few of the more popular roses available as standards are 'Apricot Nectar' (soft, perfumed apricot flowers;), 'Iceberg'

(white), 'Mr Lincoln' (deep red) and 'Queen Elizabeth' (pink). Weeping standards are normally grafted onto 2 m (6 ft) tall rootstock; 'Buff Beauty', 'Dorothy Perkins' and 'Edna Walling'

LEFT: *Ficus pumila (Climbing Fig) is an easily maintained evergreen climber with oval to heart-shaped leaves. It has been neatly clipped to give a formal look to this this small half-moon pond.*

BELOW: *In front of the Japanese Maple is a hedge of* Camellia sasanqua, *a very versatile garden shrub. It is a quick-growing species and at maturity can be pruned to shape as a hedge. Flowers bloom from autumn to early winter.*

are three beauties. For the very tiny formal setting, a miniature standard may be preferred. 'Little Red Devil' (cherry red), 'Queen Margarethe' (soft pink, larger flowers), 'Snow Carpet' (white), and 'The Fairy' (pink) are a few notables from the wide range available.

Apart from roses, some of the smaller citrus (such as mandarin and cumquat) lend themselves to clipping as standards, as do *Laurus nobilis* (Bay Tree) and *Fuchsia*.

Dendranthema frutescens (Marguerite Daisy) makes a charming standard specimen; a potted pair of these daisies can act as sentinels flanking a door or entrance way.

Camellias, especially the *C. japonica* group, retain the neat, tight habit so desirable in a formal garden. The flowers also suit the genre, most notably the formal doubles which are of a regular form with many layers of petals

symmetrically arranged around the centre bud. 'Blushing Beauty' (white-edged pale pink), 'Philippa Ifould' (soft peach pink), 'Prince Eugene Napoleon' (deep red) and 'Prince Frederick William' (soft pink) are beautiful selections.

Also of neat rounded habit are hydrangeas. Rather than attempting to keep larger ones low by severe annual pruning, choose hybrids of low compact habit such as 'Ami Pasquier', which has deep and richly coloured flowers. 'Carmen' is dwarf in habit to 0.5 m (1½ ft), free flowering with fringed petals. 'Nixe' is also small in stature and has either carmine red or violet blue flower heads, depending on the pH of the soil supporting it. 'Rubis' grows a little taller, to the 1 m (3 ft) mark, with large florets of ruby red or violet.

When choosing plants for a small formal garden, especially when selecting a plant for an urn or planter in a focal point, consider the many dwarf conifers available. They are relatively pest free and are at their best throughout all seasons, making them good selections for such a purpose. *Chamaecyparis obtusa* 'Nana Gracilis' and *C. o.* 'Nana Aurea' both suit pot culture.

Edging plants assume great importance in the formal setting, and there are other suitable and stylish plants apart from the low hedging plants such as box. A line of dwarf *Agapanthus* makes an effective edging to a paved path, as does the annual *Bellis perennis* (English Daisy). Likewise a thick ribbon planting of *Polemonium caeruleum* (Jacob's Ladder), or *Zephyranthes* (Autumn Crocus) flanking a straight path or edging a square bed would prove stunning.

THE COMPACT COTTAGE GARDEN

Romantic cottage gardens are filled with flowering annuals, perennials, roses, bulbs and herbs together with pretty climbers scrambling over arches and arbours. To most people the traditional cottage garden conjures up images of thatch-roofed cottages, walls covered with honeysuckle and roses, and gardens where *Clematis*, forget-me-nots, pansies, pinks, hollyhocks, marigolds and a hundred other herbs and flowers grow in sweet and colourful profusion. This style perfectly suits today's smaller gardens, providing year-round interest with displays of colour and foliage and the heavenly scents of summer.

LEFT: *An arbour is the perfect structure with which to create cottage-garden flavour.*

Romantic cottage gardens are filled with flowering annuals, perennials, roses, bulbs and herbs together with pretty climbers scrambling over arches and arbours.

Historically, the cottage garden was a place to grow plants for medicinal, culinary and aromatic purposes. Useful plants were nevertheless charming, with *Digitalis purpurea* (Foxglove), *Papaver* species (Poppy), *Lychnis shalcedonica* (Campion), *Primula vulgaris* (Primrose), *Lunaria annua* (Honesty) and *Viola odorata* (Sweet Violet) vying for attention. Even today, productive plants should not be overlooked in the planting scheme of a cottage garden.

Although cottage gardens should never appear formal or regimented, in very small city gardens it is

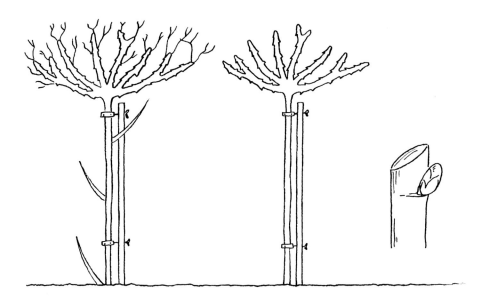

LEFT: *Prune standard roses in early spring so that the stems that form the head of the tree are almost equal in length and form an open vase shape. Use sharp secateurs and cut at a slant 7–8 mm (⅓ in.) above a healthy bud, making sure that the bud is pointing in the direction of the desired growth. Prune any side shoots along the main stem below the head, or at the base, as close to the stem as possible. Remove any dead or diseased wood and any crossed or tangled stems.*

undoubtedly better to keep the basic design structure clean and unfussy whilst having the planting itself exuberant and abundant in the cottage style. The smaller the garden, the less uncluttered the 'hard' landscape features should be.

When planting a small cottage-style garden aim for abundance of foliage and flower, a riot of colour and scent, only limited by the imagination. Small sites demand small-scale plants. Avoid huge unwieldily species that are capricious in growth and likely to invade the entire garden.

Certain old-fashioned flowers have become associated with cottage gardening. These include *Alcea* (Hollyhock), *Aloysia* (Lemon Verbena), *Aquilegia* (Granny's Bonnet), *Calendula* (Pot Marigold), *Cheiranthus* (Wallflower), *Crocus*, *Dianthus* (Sweet William), *Fritillaria*, *Galanthus* (Snowdrop), *Matthiola* (Stock), *Narcissus*, *Nigella* (Love-in-a-Mist), *Primula* (Primrose), *Rosa* (Rose), *Tropaeolum* (Nasturtium), and *Viola* (Violet). Today all these plants can be used to brighten gardens. For many there are improved versions, but plant the best of the old-fashioned varieties, too, to help achieve the right effect.

Herbs, such as angelica, balm and thyme, are also a part of traditional cottage gardens.

Rather than broadcasting the seeds, plant in definite groups, grading colours and sizes. Use plants that self-seed, such as *Cosmos bipinnatus* (Cosmos), *Consolida* (Larkspur), *Euphorbia marginata* (Snow-on-the-Mountain) and *Lunaria annua* (Honesty). Merge one group with the next.

For tall accents, *Digitalis purpurea* (Foxglove) is unsurpassed. Although perennial, it is best treated as an annual; its self-seeding habit endears it to gardeners by providing many plants for little money. The 'Foxy' strain, semi-dwarf in habit (to 1.2 m/ 4 ft), is suitable for background

bedding in the tiny cottage garden.
Other tall feature plants include
Consolida (Larkspur), *Helianthus* species
(Sunflower), *Centaurea cyanus* (Corn-
flower, also 'Baby Blue' to 30 cm/
1 ft), *Campanula medium* (Canterbury
Bell), and *Cosmos bipinnatus* (Cosmos).

For midheight fillers choose from
Dendranthema maxima (Shasta Daisy),
Dendranthema frutescens (Marguerite
Daisy), *Lupinus* species (Lupin),
Rudbeckia hirta (Cone Flower),
Heliotropium (Cherry Pie) and *Verbena*.

Aster frikarti adds a dainty touch to
a garden picture, with its lavender
daisy flowers. *Aquilegia* (Granny's
Bonnet), so beloved in cottage
gardens, come in assorted colours
and heights. The McKana hybrids
are possibly the best known, but
smaller types such as 'Mini Star' and
the 'Music' series are of compact,
dwarf habit which suit tiny gardens
or pots. *Platycodon* (Balloon Flower)
is a delightful, purple-flowered,
herbaceous perennial which adds

charm to any garden during summer.
The species will fill out to about
50 cm (20 in.) high and wide but
P. 'Misato Dwarf' is an excellent
substitute for a stunning effect in
areas of limited space.

Low carpeting plants that soften
the edges of beds and spill onto
paths are important additions,
contributing to the charm and
delight of the relaxed cottage style.
Convolvulus mauritanicus (Ground
Morning Glory), the pretty purple

LEFT: *Certain old-
fashioned flowers have
become associated with
cottage gardening, such
as this Aquilegia hybrid
(Granny's Bonnet, or
Columbine).*

It is important to account for sun and shade tolerance when making plant selections. Hydrangeas (Hortensias and Lacecaps), *Bergenia cordifolia* (Saxifraga), *Helleborus orientalis* (Lenten Rose) and *Abutilon* are all plants suited to a cottage style and most comfortable growing in shaded positions. Likewise, many cottage plants thrive in a sunny aspect — lavender, roses, annuals and most perennials.

Bulbs are a seasonal highlight in all gardens, be it cottage or formal, large or small. Many species of bulb will easily fit into the tiniest of spaces and most take kindly to pot culture. *Anemone, Ranunculus, Leucojum* and *Narcissus* (daffodils and jonquils) spring to mind when picturing a cottage setting.

Very petite growers such as *Zephyranthes candida* (Autumn Crocus), *Muscari botryoides* (Grape Hyacinth), and *Ipheion uniflorum* (Spring Star-flower) should be given preference where a low, tight, bunching effect is desired.

ABOVE AND RIGHT: *Metal arches and lattice work are traditional features of cottage-garden design, where no space is wasted.*

daisy *Brachycombe, Arenaria montana* (Sandwort) and *Lobularia maritima* (Alyssum, or Sweet Alice) all produce a softening effect. Any of these can also be treated as a spillover from raised beds or small rock gardens. For this purpose also consider either *Abutilon megapotamicum* or *Gaura lindheimeri,* both graceful in habit, lending a light touch to a landscape picture.

Tripod, lattice work and metal arches are common features of cottage design. They can support a variety of climbers, from roses to flowering vines. It is vital, where space is critically limited, to clothe such supports with a well-behaved plant that won't escape or require constant pruning. *Lathyrus odoratus* (Sweet Pea), planted in early autumn, will give the desired effect of dazzling flowers and heady fragrance without overwhelming any structure.

A cottage garden would not be complete without roses. Standards, weeping standards, climbers and bushes are all suitable. Avoid modern Hybrid Tea and Floribundas, and choose from old-fashioned varieties. Some lusty types will swell out of bounds in gardens the size of pocket-handkerchiefs, so be sure to select ones of appropriate habit. 'Crepuscule', 'Perle d'Or', 'Souvenir de la Malmaison' and 'The Portland Rose' are all excellent candidates. Alternatively, choose one of the roses of more vigorous growth which is available grafted as a weeping standard, making it much more manageable in limited areas. 'Buff Beauty', 'Dorothy Perkins' and 'Sea Foam' are all available as such.

David Austin, an English hybridiser, has developed many roses of unparalleled beauty by combining old roses with modern kinds. They have the same habit as old-fashioned flowers; many of which are perfumed and they're ideal for the modern cottage garden. 'Canterbury', 'Othello', 'Prospero', 'Tamora', 'The Squire', 'Wife of Bath', 'Wise Portia' and 'Yellow Button' will all keep to within a height of 1 m (3 ft).

LEFT: *Sundials add an instant cottage-garden touch to a small area.*

GOOD SOIL

Soil enrichment is important, as quality of the soil directly affects the health and growth of the plants it supports.

The object is to produce a rich, nourishing soil that is easily broken (friable), does not form a crust, permits water to enter freely and drain easily, and allows easy cultivation and effortless removal of weeds.

Many soils do not naturally have this type of structure, but they can be improved by regularly adding organic matter (for example, manure, and composted plant and vegetable wastes).

Clay soils can be improved with organic matter and by mixing coarse sand with the top soil.

❦ A Mediterranean Courtyard

If you are living in an area where dry, hot summers are followed by cool, fairly moist winters then you're living in an area eminently suited to a Mediterranean-style garden.

Features of the Mediterranean garden include the development of cool, quiet, enclosed spaces acting as havens from the outside heat, hustle and bustle; hard surfaces and architectural structures dominating yet softened by leafy plants and vines; the use of water features to

RIGHT: *Sizeable terracotta pots and tubs can be planted with fruiting cumquat or other citrus trees to add a distinctly Mediterranean quality.*

BELOW RIGHT: *Terracotta edgings around a flower bed can add a Mediter-ranean flavour to your garden or patio.*

bring a subtle and harmonious dimension to the otherwise severe structure and predominantly sunny, dry atmosphere; and the incorporation of terracotta pots and tubs for container planting. It is a splendidly sophisticated style, based on rigid landscaping made pleasurable by the overlay of water and greenery, and courtyards and patios are capable of being styled in this genre.

The Mediterranean garden traces its origins back to the influence of the Moors. Walled enclosures were designed to provide a tranquil relief from long, hot, arid summers. Features included tiled surfaces, vines grown over pergolas to create dappled, soothing shade below, and fountains, cascades of running water, and ornamental pools or ponds.

The prevalence of pavers, stone and gravel lends a 'hard' feeling to Mediterranean gardens, relative to other garden styles, but this quality is softened and given texture by a range of delightful evergreen plants, climbers, bulbs, annuals and potted specimens. Although a lawn area is possible, it reduces the authenticity of the style and is rarely satisfactory, mainly because grass will not grow well in dry summer areas unless it is artificially watered.

Plant possibilities and gardening systems to consider are the clever placement of pots, the incorporation of raised beds, and the utilisation of wall space. It is worth noting that warmth of a microclimate can be increased if an area is bordered by walls absorbing the sun's warmth by day and releasing it by night. This

has ramifications where the garden style holds great appeal but the region under consideration is cooler than a Mediterranean climate demands. Wall treatments can include lattice or espalier. All manner of fruiting trees can be espaliered, and for softening lattice work choose from *Bougainvillea*, *Mandevilla sanderi* (Red Brazilian

BELOW: This courtyard is dominated by the hard surfaces of white walls and terracotta tiles, but is softened by the clever placement of leafy plants in tubs and pots.

POLLUTION AND PLANTS

City dwellers are faced daily with the problem of pollutants in the air, water and soil. Common pollutants include sulphur dioxide, smoke, and fumes from motor vehicles. The effects on gardens can be minimised by choosing plant species that are tolerant of atmospheric pollution.

In general, deciduous plants are less likely to be affected than evergreen plants. Deciduous plants lose and renew their foliage annually and are therefore more likely to cope with a build up of toxins. (Exceptions to this are *Betula* species (Birch), *Malus* species (Apples, Crab Apples), *Pyrus* species (Pear), and some *Acer* species that are susceptible to different types of pollutants.)

Type of leaf can be a guide to plant choice. For example, smooth, waxy leaves are less likely to have their pores clogged with solid particles in the air than leaves that have sticky, hairy surfaces, or those that have a thin cuticle and large numbers of stomata (breathing pores) on the surface.

Plants considered tolerant of air pollution are some of the *Pittosporum* species, *Westringia frutisoca*, *Coprosma repens* (Looking-glass Plant), *Mesembry-anthemum* species, *Lantana camara* hybrids, *Lantana montevidensis* and *Nerium oleander* (Oleander).

Look around the gardens and parks in your area to see which plants are growing happily amid the city pollution. A local nursery will be able to advise you on plants that are suitable for your area.

Jasmine) or *Solanum jasminoides* (White Potato Vine).

Terracotta urns are impressive left empty and simply placed as a feature, or filled with cascading trailers such as *Convolvulus mauritanicus* (Ground Morning Glory), *Campanula portenschlagiana* (Bellflower) or *Cerastium tomentosum* (Snow in Summer).

Sizeable terracotta pots and tubs can be planted with quite dramatic plants, such as *Datura* (Angels Trumpet), *Strelitzia reginae*, *Arbutus unedo* (Irish Strawberry Tree) or *Robinia*, or with fruiting citrus trees. Supplement these large feature pots with regular sized ones to add an interesting mixture of sizes and shapes.

Subtle evergreens are indispensable in a Mediterranean-style garden: *Myrtus communis* (Common Myrtle), *Nerium oleander*

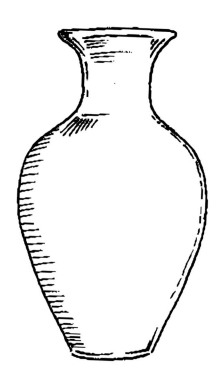

(Oleander), rosemary, lavender, *Laurus nobilis* (Bay Tree), *Viburnum tinus* (Viburnum), or *Choisya ternata* (Mexican Orange Blossom).

Potted *Pelargonium* (Geranium) is vital to creating a Mediterranean touch. Other perennials suited to the style are *Agapanthus, Clivia, Dietes, Canna, Felicia, Erigeron* (Fleabane), *Gazania* and *Osteospermum*. All manner of colourful annuals ensure the style is retained; look also to the new perennial petunia as well as the old annual type.

When choosing bulbs select from those native to the region, or at least choose from the range that appreciate similar climatic conditions and prosper in hot summers — *Vallota* and *Amaryllis belladonna* are two stalwarts.

The Mediterranean courtyard style offers scope for busy people to create a simple, uncluttered garden requiring only minimum care. In addition, it is perfect for those desiring a leafy outdoor room in which to relax and entertain.

This type of courtyard does not demand a lot of space: a small area of about 5 square metres (50 square feet) is adequate for establishing a courtyard in this manner.

The establishment of the area may initially prove expensive — with wall building, paving and erecting pergolas — but afterwards there will be little cost in terms of money and time. A Mediterranean courtyard is one of the least time consuming in terms of tending plants and garden maintenance.

The 'walled' effect also creates the privacy so necessary in the inner city area where the density of housing is greatest, and the necessity to create one's own private space becomes paramount.

ABOVE: *A Mediterranean courtyard does not need a lot of space and provides a welcome haven from the harsh summer heat.*

ABOVE: *A beautiful spring arrangement of terracotta pots and elegant statuary.*

NEAR RIGHT: *In very small gardens, where space is at a premium, it is useful to incorporate plants that will occupy vertical space. Jasminum polyanthum (Sweet-scented Jasmine) is a vigorous climber.*

FAR RIGHT: *Dainty white primulas dress up a stark window ledge.*

❧ THE POTTED GARDEN

In city gardens the size of pocket-handkerchiefs the entire plant collection may be devoted to pots, bearing semblance to verdant landscapes without actually having to dig beds and provide substantial ground space. In gardens with a little more space, pots can be used to supplement in-ground plantings.

Potted plants can be used as accent plants at focal points such as corners, the ends of vistas, or at spots where paths intersect; they can transform a bare expanse of wall or

(a size to match its dimensions) and is provided with the right growing conditions (potting media, water, light, air and fertiliser).

Choices may be made from a range of several groups: deciduous and evergreen trees or shrubs, citrus or other fruit trees, conifers, roses,

LEFT: Clematis cascades from an urn.

BELOW: For pots, Ficus species are hard to surpass and perform best when they are a little root-bound.

fence; and they can be grouped together for mass displays.

Beautiful large pots containing specimen plants make striking accents at the top or bottom of stairways, and a pair can be used attractively as sentinels for doors, gates and arches.

A potted garden includes standing pots, hanging baskets, and window boxes, and allows plants to be grown in almost any position and at any height. A potted garden allows you to move plants about very easily, which you will want to do when a plant has finished flowering or drops its leaves or is cut back. Potted plants can also be moved in and out of shelter as the weather allows.

When selecting plants to grow in containers, be mindful that almost any plant can be housed in this way for a considerable period of time, as long as it is given enough root space

PLANTING TRADITIONAL STRAWBERRY POTS

A terracotta strawberry pot makes a charming container, especially for herbs, and there is a technique to using them successfully.

First, as with all terracotta pots, give the empty pot a good soaking in a bucket of water so that the pot will not immediately draw moisture from the potting soil. When the last air bubble has risen to the surface, you are ready to begin potting.

Fill the pot with potting soil up to the level of the first pocket. Working *within* the pot, plant the roots of the first herb into the soil and poke the leaves out of the pocket. Firm down the roots with your hand.

Fill the pot with soil up to the level of the next pocket, and plant the second herb. Continue in this way until all the pockets (and the top) are filled.

Water slowly and gently, taking care that the water percolates through the potting soil rather than merely runs out the pockets.

(If you had filled the entire pot with soil and then tried to poke the plant roots through the pockets — that is, from the outside to the inside — the plants would most likely have been dislodged with the first watering.)

Suitable plants for the pockets of the strawberry pot are bushy types and trailing types (for example, basil and thyme. For the top of the pot, a plant of low to medium height would be an attractive choice (for example, chives and parsley).

perennials, bulbs, orchids, succulents, palms, ferns and annuals. Personal preference and suitability to the overall style of the garden, along with suitability to local climate, will be paramount considerations. Time available to look after potted plants will also affect choices made; if time is minimal, select types that don't require daily tending and annual repotting.

A potted garden provides a wonderful opportunity to make a statement about the grower's personality and the ambience of their outdoor living area. When selecting plants suitable for container gardening, avoid those cast-iron but overused plants, such as philodendrons, dracaenas or other 'shopping centre' or 'office' plants. Creativity and imagination can be bought to the fore and a highly personal and attractive landscape can be formed.

STANDING POTS

Most annuals perform favourably when contained in pots, making pretty additions to any outdoor situation. Match the annual to the pot: spillovers suit urns and dishes, whereas upright types look better in traditional vase-shaped pots. Mix and match annuals for a colourful arrangement or overplant seasonal bulbs with them for stunning effect. *Lobularia maritima* (Alyssum, or Sweet Alice), *Ageratum houstonianum* (Floss Flower), *Malcolmia maritima* (Virginia Stock), *Primula* species (Fairy Primrose), *Nemophila menziesi* (Baby Blue Eyes) and *Lobelia* all suit this purpose well. Standard roses, citrus or evergreens look pretty when underplanted with these same annuals. Other annuals commonly used for pots are petunias, nasturtiums and polyanthus.

Azaleas adapt beautifully to pots and make impressive spring pictures when massed. They do need attention — watering, fertilising, pruning, deadheading, and spraying for petal fungal disease and leaf-spoiling insects — however, most growers regard them as worthy of the effort. There are numerous forms and cultivars supporting many different flower colours, but it is hard to surpass the white ones. The smaller Kurumes and Gumpos take to smaller pots, whilst the larger Belgian hybrids and tall Indicas will require more root space at maturity and demand a larger tub.

Avoid planting an azalea in a cement container, as the lime content in the cement can leach into the soil and may kill the plant, or make it very unhappy at any rate. Alternatively, line the cement pot with heavy duty plastic prior to potting up, ensuring that a hole is cut in the plastic corresponding with the drainage hole. All containers must be very well-drained, as azaleas suffer badly if they are waterlogged.

are more easily controlled; in the open garden it often fails because the soil is unsuitable. The fragrance is unforgettable. Prune after flowering to produce a longer-lived and healthier bush.

The sweetly scented gardenia is a beautiful pot plant perfect for the temperate or subtropical gardener. The snow-white, waxy flowers, with their delicious perfume, bloom in spring and summer. When not in flower the gardenia is still attractive, having shiny, mid-green leaves and a pleasing, bushy appearance. Potted gardenias can be brought inside at the height of flowering to savour their beauty and fragrance indoors.

Fragrant lavender is wonderfully aromatic, it makes an excellent pot plant and is well-suited to life in a window box. It will grow in most climates, except in the tropics.

ABOVE AND RIGHT: Match the plant to its pot. Spillovers suit urns and dishes; upright types look better in vase shapes.

Scent is always an added attraction in a garden, and there are many perfumed plant species that are equally at home in-ground or contained. *Boronia megastigma* (Brown Boronia) actually performs better in a pot, where its cultural conditions

can be at hand to receive first rate attention from the grower, as well as being situated for optimum viewing. Daffodils, jonquils and tulips make a cheerful scene in the cooler regions; the 'Hoop Petticoat' daffodils are especially suited to smaller pots and

LEFT AND BELOW: *Of the many plants that grow happily in pots, some of the most beautiful are* Impatiens, Convolvulus mauritanicus, *roses and sweet peas.*

Michelia figo (Port Wine Magnolia) makes a handsome potted plant. Ideally it should be placed near an entrance or doorway in order to get the full impact of its fruity, delicious fragrance. It rarely exceeds 2 m (6 ft) in a container, is densely clothed with glossy leaves, and bears inconspicuous spring flowers that emit a heady, fruity scent rather like old-fashioned port wine. Its attractive, compact habit is suited to a deep formal tub.

Other perfumed plants which take kindly to pot culture are roses, Daphne, herbs and scented-leafed pelargoniums.

Bulbs are delightful seasonal features whether in-ground or potted. The first shoots poking up through the cold, late winter ground bring a feeling of wonder and expectation. Most bulbs grow beautifully in containers, where they troughs. *Muscari* (Grape Hyacinths), being small in stature, clump up nicely in confined spaces, as does *Ipheion uniflorum* (Spring Star-flower). Choose *Anemone* and *Ranunculus* for a bright splash of colour, and freesias or hyacinths for fragrance. For something a little different, consider some of the *Allium* (Onion) family, *Lachenalia* (Cape Cowslip) or one of the many lovely species of *Crocus*.

For a reliable outdoor summer display of delightful flowers, consider *Dendranthema frutescens* (Marguerite Daisy), which performs admirably in a pot. It will form a shrubby bush laden with masses of white, yellow or pink flowers. It needs ample soil, so plant it in a deep tub. The bush will eventually be wider than it is high, and even when not flowering, the shapely mass of green, deeply cut foliage is attractive. It likes full sun and will continue to flower almost all year round as long as spent blooms are deadheaded. Nipping off blooms will also promote bushy growth.

Hydrangeas also provide a reliable outdoor display of blue, mauve, pink or white flowers in summer. They grow very well in pots (where it is easier to control flower colour than in the garden). Acid soil supports blue flowers, and alkaline soil, pink. White flowers remain white. Choose from Hortensias (large globe-shaped flower clusters) and Lacecaps (a ring of flowers surrounding a hump of smaller flowers). Hydrangeas in pots will perform best in the light shade.

Autumn and winter are seasons when people hanker for flower colour to bring interest to their gardens, although autumn could hardly be called dull with such spectacular foliage colour abounding in cooler regions.

Camellias will bring floral interest in those times of the year when it is most needed. Young plants are wonderful in pots, progressing to large tubs at maturity. (A young camellia shouldn't be planted in a tub that is too large for

sun and the roots are kept cool and protected by a surface mulch.

Don't overlook the value of palms and ferns when decorating outdoor living areas with potted plants. They bring a cool, unfussy restfulness to landscapes, with interest focussed on leaf shape and green colour tonings rather than floral value.

In a fundamentally green garden bereft of flowering shrubs, the addition of variegated foliaged

LEFT AND BELOW: *Citrus trees will grow happily in tubs, as will primulas.*

it, as the unused soil will quickly become sour and probably too wet.)

Camellia japonica possesses a rather formal beauty, being a tidy and elegant plant. Flowers range from formal, informal, single and double flowers in colours of red, white, pink, rose or mauve to a combination of these and similar shades. *C. sasanqua* can also be potted. It will tolerate more sun than *C. japonica* and it is not such a dense shrub. Camellia foliage is mid to dark green, slightly shiny, and even when the flowers are not in bloom the shrub looks fresh and attractive.

Most camellias prefer the semi-shade of the outdoors, as the early morning's direct sun can scorch the flowers (some varieties — mainly the reds — are not so sensitive). Camellias are best suited to temperate and cool regions. They can be grown in some warm areas if the blooms are protected from the

RIGHT: *A cheerful spot in a shady courtyard: a pot of* Impatiens *and a little white pig.*

BELOW: *A formal arrangement of pots in a courtyard acquires depth by the clever addition of a mirror.*

a little pot bound. It will spread to around 3 m (10 ft) with shiny green foliage and waxy, star-shaped clusters of fragrant pink flowers. Other climbers which appreciate being potted are *Solanum jasminoides* (White Potato Vine), *Trachelospermum jasminoides, Stephanotis floribunda, Mandevilla sanderi* (Red Brazilian Jasmine) and *Gelsemium sempervirens.*

Potted standards and topiary make a real fashion statement. Arrangements can be created by combining clipped trees and shrubs with terracotta or grey cement pots and urns, tasteful statuary, water features and brass fittings. The best species for clipping is undoubtedly *Buxus* species, but ivy trains well onto wire frames and *Laurus nobilis* (Bay Tree), *Fuchsia, Dendranthema frutescens* (Marguerite Daisy), roses and *Bougainvillea* can all be trained as standards. Some of the smaller conifers with compact and uniform habits also suit this purpose well.

ABOVE: *An old cast-iron bath makes an excellent container for a luxuriant massing of leafy plants.*

FAR LEFT: *This dwarf date palm and cycad bring a cool, unfussy restfulness to a courtyard.*

NEAR LEFT: *In gardens with a little more space, pots can be used to supplement in-ground plantings.*

HANGING BASKETS

Hanging baskets are ideal for the city garden and make a graceful adornment to pergolas, verandahs, sunrooms and balconies.

An enormous range of basket styles is available, from the traditional wire variety to smart ceramic containers, half baskets that fit flush against walls, and practical plastic models equipped with drainage saucers.

Plants in hanging baskets need some special consideration. They require a high-quality soil mix, as they need to take all their nutrients from the small amount of soil in the basket. It is possible to buy hanging basket mixtures as well as indoor plant mixtures, and both are suitable.

Plants in baskets hung outdoors need more water than stationary, ground-level pots, as they are exposed to constant evaporation on all sides. To retain moisture, choose baskets made of impervious materials, or line wire baskets with sphagnum moss, or with ready-made liners of coconut fibre, bark or wool, and then give them an inner lining of plastic — with drainage holes punched through the base — baskets will not only last longer, but will retain the attractive appearance of natural materials.

Recognise the needs of the plant and water moderately but regularly, preferably in the morning. Plants should be kept consistently just damp, not wet.

Care will have to be taken with the sun, as the soil in a basket can easily suffer a reduction in moisture and an increase in temperature. Plants in hanging baskets are often happier in semi-shaded areas, especially in summer.

Plant arrangement

Trailing plants, such as ferns and flowering creepers, are particularly suited to hanging baskets, and their grouping and arrangement should be

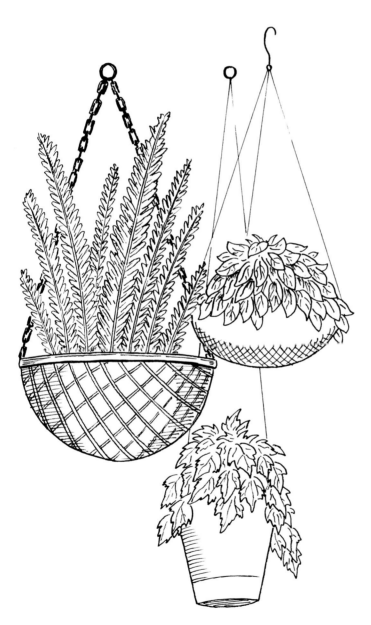

carefully planned for the most effective display.

Baskets look more attractive hung in groups rather than singly, and they look best when hung at different heights. Baskets featuring flowering plants need to be hung lower than baskets with trailing plants so that the blooms can be seen. To disguise the wire, chain or rope from which the basket hangs, place a soft-foliaged (for example, maidenhair or fishbone fern) or twining plant above and behind the flowering one.

Plain and variegated leafed plants, when mixed together in groupings can provide an interesting and attractive contrast.

Plants of differing heights, colours and textures growing together in the one basket create an abundant and pleasing effect.

For hanging foliage, consider the following: *Adiantum* species (Maidenhair Fern), *Ceropegia woodi* (Chain of Hearts), *Cissu antarctica* (Kangaroo Vine), *Davallia* species (Hare's Foot Fern), *Hedera* species (Ivy), *Pellionia* species (Rainbow Vine), *Peperomia* species (Peperomia), *Pilea* species (Aluminium Plant), *Plectranthus australis* (Swedish Ivy) and *Tolmiea menziesi* (Piggyback Plant).

For hanging flowers, consider the following: *Aeschynanthus pulcher* (Lipstick Plant), *Campanula portenschlagiana* (Bellflower), *Convolvulus mauritanicus* (Ground Morning Glory), *Fuchsia* species (trailing types), *Heterocentron elegans* (Spanish Shawl), *Hoya bella* (Wax Plant), *Pelargonium peltatum* (Ivy Geranium), *Petunia* hybrids (annual cascading cultivars or perennial Petunia), *Rhodanthe anthemoides* (syn. *Helipterum anthemoides*) (Paper Daisy) and *Tropaeolum majus* (Nasturtium),

WINDOW BOXES

Window boxes, generously filled with lush greenery or colourful flowering plants, can provide much needed garden space for flat dwellers or increase existing garden space in tiny urban gardens.

Window boxes are ideal places for trailing plants. Ivy, geraniums, *Convolvulus mauritanicus* (Ground Morning Glory), *Rosmarinus lavandulaceus* (Prostrate Rosemary), trailing annuals, and the perennial petunia are suitable for the sunny spots in your garden; ivy, *Vinca minor* and *Trachelospermum jasminoides* will grow heartily in the shade.

Being elevated and exposed to the elements on all sides means the potting mix in the planter will dry

ABOVE: *A conservatory window is filled with a brilliant display of potted plants.*

RIGHT: *For a spot that does not receive too much sun, you might consider pots of tuberous begonias.*

being rested in shady areas of the house or garden and are tolerant of cool temperatures.

Flowering bulbs massed in ceramic pots make wonderful short term indoor highlights. They should be kept inside while the flowers last and then discarded or planted out in the garden where they may produce flowers the following year. Some, such as *Lachenalia* (Cape Cowslip), *Hippeastrum* and *Vallota* (Scarborough Lily) will flower again the following year if kept in pots. Daffodils, jonquils, tulips, hyacinths and lily-of-the-valley will all perform well for one season.

Bulbs like a well-lit position close to a window, but little or no direct sunlight. They will thrive at normal room temperature with good ventilation. Cooler conditions will result in longer-lasting flowers. When buying potted bulbs from the nursery, look for plants with flowers just coming into bloom. If you are choosing daffodils, note that the flowers and stems of small daffodils (such as 'Hoop Petticoat') are less likely to topple over than the taller-growing ones.

When the flowers are spent, if you wish to plant the bulbs into the garden, tip the bulbs and their soil out of the pot, and plant them in the garden. Continue watering them until the foliage yellows, then gradually lessen the amount until leaves are dead. With those to be kept in pots, allow the soil to dry

LEFT: Vallota (Scarborough Lily) is easy to grow and ideally suited to a warm and sunny position.

BELOW: Mexican sage, marigolds and flowering chives. When their blooms are spent, other flowering plants can take their place on the window sill.

DRY AIR

Container plants are especially vulnerable to moisture loss, and indoor plants are no exception. Their moisture requirements will need to be monitored.

The plant will also be affected by the material of which its pot is made. Terracotta pots are porous, and this means that they will draw moisture from the potting soil. Plastic and glazed ceramic pots are waterproof, so the potting soil will not dry out as fast. Plants in terracotta pots will, therefore, require watering more frequently.

A good way of testing whether your plant needs water is to put your finger a little way into the potting soil (say 2 cm/1 in.). The top of the soil may feel dry, but the soil underneath may in fact be damp.

When you water your indoor plants, water them deeply. The danger of watering them little and often is that their roots will stay near the surface. Don't let your plants sit in a dish of water, however, as they will become soggy. Let the water drain freely from the pot after watering.

If the air indoors is very dry (as is common in air-conditioned and heated rooms), stand the pot in a dish of pebbles or gravel and add water (making sure the base of the pot doesn't touch the water). Another method of adding humidity to the air is to spray the plants with mist (a refillable spray bottle is ideal).

out as the leaves wither. Repot them with fresh potting mix after their dormancy, in readiness for the next season.

Other popular flowering house plants include *Sinningia speciosa* (Gloxinia), which blooms well in diffused sunlight indoors. Their clusters of velvety bell-shaped flowers are quite spectacular. Although gloxinias are normally purchased for short-term decoration they can be retained for a further season if, after flowering, water is withheld until the soil is quite dry. When the plant dies down, remove the dead foliage and store the tuber (still in the pot) on its side in a cool dark place for 3 months. When ready to start the plant again, replace the top 3 cm (1 in.) of soil with fresh potting mix and give the plant normal care.

African violets are much loved and widely cultivated indoor flowering plants. To achieve good results, water from below so as not to wet the sensitive foliage. They must have bright but indirect light; it is often a matter of moving the plant around until a suitable position is found. A good place is often near a window providing strong light (but not the hot blazing sun) filtered by a blind or curtain.

Cyclamens, too, are valued indoor plants. They have distinctive and elegant flowers, with reflexed petals, plain or frilled in white, deep red or any of a wide range of pinks and mauves. Plants are available from nurseries in early winter, when the first buds open. They should continue flowering for 6 to 8 weeks or more, and then remain decorative for another month or longer, until the leaves begin to wither and turn yellow. For optimum performance, keep the soil of cyclamens on the dry side and keep the plant in a cool well-lit position.

Tuberous begonias, *Spathiphyllum* (White Sails) and *Streptocarpus* (Cape Primrose) are other flowering beauties that adapt easily to conditions indoors. Tuberous begonias are rather like cyclamens and gloxinias in that they can be bought as disposable plants or kept for a further season by being given special treatment after dying down. *Spathiphyllum* species are quite hardy and will last indoors for some considerable time, whilst *Streptocarpus* may have to be rotated indoors and out for continued flowering.

For orchid lovers, *Cymbidium* hybrids are available from nurseries in late winter and spring. If they are bought when first blooms open, they should last for at least 6 weeks. If, after flowering finishes, you wish to keep the plant for the following season, the old stem should be removed and the plant put outside or, if the plant can be kept in a fresh and airy spot, it could remain indoors. To produce flowers the following season, orchids need some dappled sunlight after flowering and a cool spell in winter.

❧ THE KITCHEN GARDEN, OR POTAGER

'Potager' is a French term, meaning a kitchen garden. Growing fruit and vegetables to supply the kitchen with fresh produce is a feasible proposition even in the smallest of city gardens. The entire outdoor space may be devoted to fruit and vegetable culture and, by incorporating good design strategies, a stunning effect will be achieved.

The formal tradition of the French potager may be followed, with symmetrical beds edged with low hedges and filled with wholesome seasonal vegetables. Paving between the beds is both pleasing to the eye and provides for easy access for tending and harvesting. Trellises, espalier, overflowing urns and tubs, and standard bay or citrus trees, are incorporated to create a stylish kitchen garden. Viewed from above or at ground level, this is a most pleasing garden treatment.

Alternatively, crops may be interspersed with ornamental plantings in different garden styles to add interest and variety. Not only

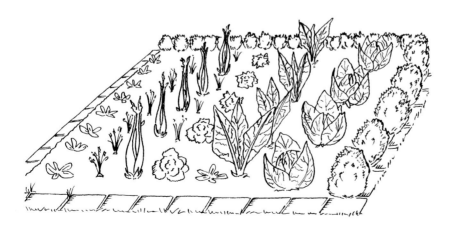

RIGHT: *Mignonette
lettuce, an ideal vegetable
for the small-scale
potager.*

BELOW: *Pink and white
ornamental kale growing
beside yellow marigolds.*

is vegetable growing suitable to the cottage style — where, traditionally, productive plants are intercropped with a profusion of flowering annuals, bulbs and perennials — but the concept can also be applied to a formal ornamental garden. Symmetrical plantings of kale or rainbow chard, edging treatments using strawberries, parsley, chives, or tubbed mandarin trees, are innovative ways to incorporate edible plants into a formal ornamental setting. Vegetables are easily accommodated in the herb garden, where the advantages of companion planting can be fully utilised to achieve good results.

To create a Mediterranean feel, consider planting appropriate vegetables in terracotta pots and make a feature of them. In this way even the smallest courtyard or balcony garden can be styled to supply fresh and healthy produce for the kitchen.

To save space in small gardens, utilise vertical areas by trellising, espaliering or planting over pergolas and arches. Vine crops, such as passionfruit or kiwi fruit, can be

LEFT: *The espalier technique saves space in a small garden. Here, raspberries are growing on a stone wall.*

BELOW: *A vegetable garden does not have to be a separate feature — vegetables and garden plants can be inter-cropped attractively.*

trained over a pergola with as much ease as purely ornamental vines and they provide food in addition to function and beauty. Espaliered fruit trees are certainly worthy of consideration; the new 'Ballerina' range of apple trees, with their unique columnar habit, are also ideal for small gardens, tight corners, patios or balconies.

Species to avoid in very small gardens where space is at a premium are the long-term in-ground crops, such as asparagus and globe artichoke, or those very large growers that require more space than is available, such as ginger and perhaps corn.

Prior to selecting a range of seeds or seedlings, also take into consideration the following factors: personal preference, the availability and relative cost of commercially grown fruits and vegetables, and climatic suitability. It is pointless to plant species that crop heartily but are not really enjoyed by the

ABOVE: *Mint grows happily in a pot in a shady position.*

RIGHT: *A drift of flowering basil above a border of Cerastium tomentosum (Snow in Summer).*

ABOVE RIGHT: *Dill, silver-beet and white roses.*

🌿 A TRADITIONAL HERB GARDEN

Cultivating herbs is a popular form of gardening providing outdoor living spaces with a rich variety of foliage and flower colour, texture and scent. As a group, herbs are easy to grow and do not require any specialised treatment. Most take up little ground space, making them ideal for the tiny urban plot;

whether the whole garden is devoted to them, or only a small portion, is entirely a matter of choice. Herbs can be added to the vegetable plot or combined with ornamental plantings. Flat dwellers limited to a sunny windowsill for gardening will be delighted at the herbs' ease of culture in this situation. Window boxes, terracotta pots and narrow borders can all be filled with a selection of herbs, ensuring attractive and functional use of valuable space.

GARDEN PESTS

Of the insecticides available on the market, those based on pyrethrum are the safest for domestic use, are highly active, and have no residual effect.

Other safe mixtures are garlic and soap sprays, which are also easy to prepare.

Soap spray is useful against some caterpillars and other larvae. Simply mix 56 grams (2 ounces) of soap flakes (or grated, pure soap) in 5 litres (8 pints 16 fluid ounces) of hot water and allow to cool.

Garlic spray is useful against sucking insects and caterpillars. Mix 2 tablespoons of mineral oil (or liquid paraffin) with 90 grams (3 ounces) of chopped garlic cloves and let stand for 48 hours. In a separate bowl, dissolve 15 grams (½ ounce) of soap flakes (or grated, pure soap) in half a litre (16 fluid ounces) of warm water. Mix the two solutions together and strain. Try different strengths, a strong one being one part mixture to 50 parts water.

If snails are invading your garden, you could try one of the following methods: place empty half-oranges upside down on the soil (snails will congregate beneath the orange halves, and they are easily disposed of), or place a barrier (such as ash) around the affected plants to impede the snail traffic. If you can bear to drown the snails, go into the garden at night and take with you a bucket of water — pick up the snails and drop them in their watery grave.

If these measures don't work, and you need to resort to other means, please be mindful of the other creatures in your garden, such as children, pets, birds, lizards, ladybirds, worms and bees.

Drifts of one species make a fine display; the choice of plant material should be determined by the habit, leaf colour or texture or flower colour and form that is deemed desirable. In addition many herbs have the tendency to form mat-like carpets, making them excellent groundcovers, bordering paths and garden beds. For the enthusiast, however, herbs should be collected together, allocated their own special place, and treated as a garden feature.

Herbs may be planted in a formal or informal style; the former being more traditional. As landscaping small spaces demands cleaner lines, an underlying formal structure will ultimately produce better design. True devotees may be inclined to replicate the complicated knot gardens, planned on a grand scale, in Elizabethan times. These varied from small 3 m × 3 m (10 ft × 10 ft) areas to quite large ones covering 6 m × 10 m (20 ft × 30 ft) or more. Each type of herb was planted in a narrow, winding and intersecting row, so that the beds of each type wound in and out of beds of other types. Complicated knot gardens could be established today, but the high maintenance and regular care required to keep them at peak condition would be demanding and time consuming.

For simpler formal treatments, a herb garden could consist of a circular bed with a bird bath, a sun dial or a potted and clipped *Laurus nobilis* (Bay Tree) at its centre.

In predominantly square areas, the garden can be divided up into geometric sections, paved with flagging stones or aged bricks to

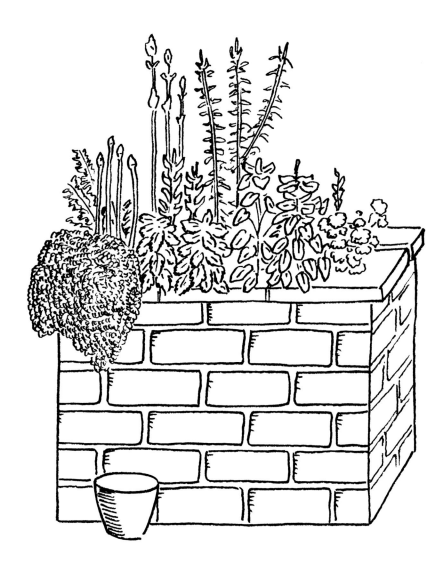

LEFT: *Herbs can be grown in the garden, in pots or in raised beds.*

give an added warmth, and lavishly planted in regular patterns. Again, a Bay Tree could be planted singly in a pot as the focal point of a square herb garden. It is also effective grown as a shrub — a pair of bays looks very attractive when grown in decorative tubs.

Bay prefers full sun, but will tolerate some shade, and is sensitive to extremely hot and cold temperatures. Moderately rich, well-drained soil will support its growth. Although tall growing if unchecked (to a 12 m/40 ft high tree in optimum conditions), it can be clipped and retained at 2 m (6 ft) or higher. To make a formal tub plant, train as a standard, and remove the side shoots and suckers from the single main stem.

Herbs suitable for a small gardens include the following: angelica, basil, borage, chives, coriander, dill, fennel, lovage, marjoram, mint, nasturtium, oregano, parsley, rosemary, sage, tarragon and thyme.

HERBS IN POTS

A large 'strawberry pot' makes an attractive and useful container for growing a selection of the smaller varieties of herbs, such as, basil, chives, chervil, marjoram, parsley, sage and thyme. A few small herbs could also be grown in a hanging basket, or in pots or troughs on a windowsill.

The herbs will need spells of fresh air outdoors, and some will need full sunlight. Angelica, borage, chives and parsley will tolerate partial shading. Mint can be grown in full shade.

Like other container plants, potted herbs will need to be watered more frequently than garden plants to stop them drying out.

Catalogue of plants suited to small gardens

For those gardeners with tiny backyards who require trees to become quickly established in order to lend a mature feeling to the landscape, see 'Quick-growing trees for gardeners in a hurry', pages 78–9.

ACER SPECIES
(MAPLES)

Deciduous; 4–5 m (13–16 ft). Suitable for containers and formal gardens; prefers full sun or partial shade.

Maples are some of the most ornamental trees suitable for gardens. Japanese Maples are outstandingly beautiful in form, leaf and autumn colour. *Acer japonicum* (the Fern-leaf Maples) and *A. palmatum* (the Japanese Maples) are suited to small spaces, and many cultivars are available.

A trip to a specialist nursery in autumn to view the range of habits and leaf colours is well worthwhile, prior to making a selection.

ALBIZIA JULIBRISSIN
(SILK TREE)

Deciduous; to 9 m (30 ft). Suitable for Mediterranean-style gardens; prefers full sun; attracts birds.

Wide spreading branches bear delicate compound leaves which fold at night. Blooms are silky balls in white and pink.

Albizia is an adaptable and pretty tree, and withstands dry conditions once established.

ARBUTUS UNEDO
(IRISH STRAWBERRY TREE)

Evergreen; to 6 m (20 ft). Suitable for formal and Mediterranean-style gardens; prefers full sun; attracts birds.

This tree has a round head, reddish bark and dark green, glossy leaves. In autumn it bears white, waxy, drooping flowers that resemble lily-of-the-valley. The flowers are followed by rounded berries that resemble strawberries. The berries remain on the tree for about ten months, turning from orange to red.

Arbutus unedo is a versatile small tree, growing well in a sunny and protected position, and will generally tolerate salt air. It will resist frost but not drought.

BACKHOUSIA CITRIODORA
(SWEET VERBENA TREE)

Evergreen; 6 m (20 ft). Suitable for Mediterranean-style gardens; prefers full sun or partial shade; attracts birds.

Backhousia can be trained to a tree shape and is delightful because of the aromatic leaves, which give off a sharp lemon scent when crushed. It bears clusters of small cream flowers in summer, which have a slight honey perfume.

Backhousia does not tolerate frost, and thrives in warm areas with ample moisture and deep rich soil.

CASSIA FISTULA
(GOLDEN SHOWER)

Deciduous; to 6 m (20 ft). Suitable for formal and Mediterranean-style gardens; prefers full sun; attracts birds.

In summer this elegant specimen tree bears fragrant, bright yellow flowers in long, drooping sprays. The large divided leaves are bright glossy green. *C. javanica* (Java Shower) is similar in habit to *C. fistula* but the flowers appear as long, drooping skeins of rose pink.

Fast growing and easily maintained for a warm, sheltered position in frost-free climates.

CLETHRA ARBOREA
(LILY-OF-THE-VALLEY TREE)

Evergreen; to 8 m (26 ft). Suitable for cottage and formal gardens; prefers partial shade; attracts birds.

From late summer to mid-autumn *Clethra* is graced with clusters of fragrant, white flowers. The deep green leaves are a perfect foil to the pretty flowers. The cultivar 'Flore-plena' bears double flowers.

Clethra arborea requires semi-shade and moist, organically enriched, acid soil. It is fast growing and easily maintained.

CORNUS FLORIDA
(FLOWERING DOGWOOD)

Deciduous; to 6 m (20 ft). Suitable for formal gardens; prefers full sun or partial shade; attracts birds.

This graceful tree's leaves that are dark green above and pale green beneath, and their autumn colourings are spectacular. The tree bears beautiful white bracts in spring, followed by red berries. Flowers in shades of pink are available in the variety 'Rubra'.

Cornus florida performs best in cool areas, is easily maintained, and prefers a moist and friable loam.

ELAEOCARPUS RETICULATUS
(BLUEBERRY ASH)

Evergreen; to 5 m (16 ft) or more. Suitable for containers; prefers full sun or partial shade; attracts birds.

This tree is attractive at all times of the year. Its bark is smooth and brown; its leaves are shiny, serrated and leathery, with prominent veins. It bears masses of fringed, white flowers followed by blue berries. The tree is pyramid-shaped when young, and rounded at maturity.

It is easily maintained and grows well in well-drained, moist loams.

GORDONIA AXILLARIS
(GORDONIA)

Evergreen; to 3–5 m (10–16 ft). Suitable for containers, cottage and formal gardens; prefers full sun or partial shade.

Gordonia is spectacular in flower in autumn through into winter. The flowers are large and creamy white with prominent gold stamens. The petals are crimped and crepe-like towards the edges.

Gordonia is very easy to grow and easily maintained. It needs a lime-free soil.

LABURNUM × WATERERI 'VOSSII'
(GOLDEN CHAIN TREE)

Deciduous; to 7 m (23 ft). Suitable for cottage and formal gardens; prefers full sun or partial shade.

This handsome small tree has spectacular spring flowers. Its bright yellow, pea-shaped flowers occur in long festoons more than 30 cm (1 ft) in length. Its leaves are grey-green and divided into three parts.

It will grow quickly in cool climates, and is easily maintained.

LAGERSTROEMIA INDICA
(CREPE MYRTLE)

Deciduous; 6–8 m (20–26 ft). Suitable for cottage, formal and Mediterranean-style gardens; prefers full sun.

This beautiful small tree has bright pink, lavender, heliotrope or white flowers. It has a naturally attractive shape, so pruning is not necessary.

It is perfect for small gardens in temperate areas, and is tolerant of light frosts.

LAURUS NOBILIS
(BAY TREE, OR BAY LAUREL)

Evergreen; to 6–7 m (20–23 ft). Suitable for containers, formal and Mediterranean-style gardens, hedges; prefers full sun.

The Bay Tree's stout main trunk divides into several upright branches. It is hardy and compact, and well-suited to clipping.

This small tree is native to the Mediterranean, and will grow well in temperate areas. It is salt-tolerant, wind-tolerant, and easily maintained.

MAGNOLIA SPECIES
(MAGNOLIA)

Deciduous and evergreen; height varies between species. Suitable for containers and formal gardens; prefers full sun or partial shade.

For small gardens, limit your choices to the smaller species. *Magnolia quinquepeta* (Lily-flowered Magnolia) reaches 4 m (13 ft) in height at maturity, forming a small tree with a short main trunk and rounded head. The species produces lilac flowers, while the cultivar *M. q.* 'Nigra' has magnificent deep ruby-red flowers. Also consider *M. stellata* (Star Magnolia) if space is restricted, as it is a shrub form. The star-shaped flowers, produced in winter, are ivory-coloured and fragrant.

M. × *soulangiana* grows taller, to 5–8 m (16–26 ft), forming an erect tree with a single trunk and low lateral branches. The large flowers are lilac outside and white inside, with a purple blotch at the base.

Magnolias are easily maintained, and prefer a deep, moist, acid soil.

MALUS SPECIES
(CRAB APPLES)

Deciduous; to 3–8 m (10–26 ft). Suitable for cottage and formal gardens; prefers full sun or partial shade; attracts birds.

Many crab apples bear fruit in late summer and autumn, following their spring flowering.

Malus × 'Gorgeous' grows to 3–4 m (10–13 ft) and has white flowers followed by large, shining, crimson fruit. 'Golden Hornet' grows to 4–5 m (13–16 ft) and has golden fruit. *M.* × *arnoldiana* grows to 4–6 m (13–20 ft) has pink flowers and yellow fruit.

M. ioensis 'Plena' (Bechtel's Crab Apple) grows to 4 m (13 ft). It does not produce fruit but it has large, pale pink, fragrant, double-flowered blooms, and its leaves colour in autumn. *M. spectabilis* 'Flore Pleno' has rose coloured, double flowers.

These and many other cultivars are suitable for cool or cool temperate climates.

PRUNUS SPECIES
(FLOWERING ALMOND, CHERRY, CHERRY-PLUM, PEACH, PLUM)

Deciduous; varying heights. Suitable for cottage and formal gardens; prefers full sun or partial shade.

Prunus are renowned for their spring floral display. Most species and cultivars are of heights truly suited to small gardens. All have a lovely sculptural winter shape when their braches are bare of leaves.

P. serrulata (Japanese Flowering Cherry) is stunning in spring. Cultivars include 'Fugenzo', which has pale pink, double flowers and grows to 8 m (26 ft); 'Kazan', which has deep pink, double flowers and grows to 6–10 m (20–33 ft); and 'Mt Fuji', which has white, pendulous, semi-double flowers and grows to 4–5 m (13–16 ft).

P. cerasifera 'Nigra' (Flowering Cherry-plum) is a popular choice for those who enjoy coloured foliage. It has deep purple leaves, pale pink flowers and grows to 4 m (13 ft) high and 3 m (10 ft) wide. For a weeping standard, select *P. subhirtella* (Weeping Rosebud Cherry), with its skirt festooned with pale pink single flowers.

In small areas where each tree or shrubs chosen must look good year-round, exclude those with dull summer foliage such as *P. persica* (Flowering Peach).

Prunus are fast growing and easily maintained, and prefer a well-drained soil.

ROBINIA PSEUDOACACIA 'FRISIA'
(FALSE ACACIA)

Deciduous; to 10 m (33 ft). Suitable for cottage, formal and Mediterranean-style gardens; prefers full sun.

This is a most effective specimen tree for a small garden. The leaves are delicate and lacy, and appear in differing shades of yellow according to the season. The flowers are pea-shaped, white and perfumed.

Robinia adapts to most soils and positions, and is frost-tolerant.

ROTHMANNIA GLOBOSA
(TREE GARDENIA)

Evergreen; to 3–4 m (10–16 ft). Suitable for containers, cottage and formal gardens; prefers full sun or partial shade.

This delightful small tree bears scented, bell-shaped, creamy white flowers throughout spring, followed by dark brown seed pods.

It is adaptable to most well-composted soils, and is resistant to drought and frosts.

TECOMA SPECIES
(TECOMA)

Evergreen; to 3–5 m (10–16 ft). Suitable for containers and Mediterranean-style gardens; prefers full sun.

The graceful *T. garrocha* has bright green, fern-like, dense foliage and grows to 3 m (10 ft). It flowers are yellow with a scarlet tube, trumped-shaped, and appear in summer and autumn.

T. stans (Yellow Elder) has fern-like foliage, grows to 5 m (16 ft) and has bright yellow flowers in summer.

Tecomas prefer warm to tropical coastal conditions with rich, well-drained soil. They are drought and frost tender.

ATTRACTING BIRDS

Birds are invaluable to a garden, large or small, adding life and beauty whilst pollinating the flowers and controlling the insects.

Birds can be attracted into your garden if you plant suitable vegetation (for food and shelter) and if you provide a sympathetic environment (including water).

If you wish to attract birds that are native to your area, select plants that provide shelter and food and are also native to your area.

Red berries and red flowers will draw birds, as will nectar-producing plants, and prickly shrubbery will provide a safe haven for bird-nesting sites.

You will be far kinder to the birds if you plant suitable vegetation rather than providing them with birdseed (or worse, honey or sugar). First, birds need to be able to forage for food, and also teach their young how to do so. Secondly, encouraging birds to eat food that is not part of their natural diet may cause dire effects (such as beak deformities and soft eggshells).

QUICK-GROWING TREES FOR GARDENERS IN A HURRY

NAME OF TREE	HEIGHT	LEAVES	FLOWERS	FRUITS
Acacia baileyana (Cootamundra Wattle)	6 m (20 ft)	Blue-grey	Bright yellow	Legume
Acer buergerianum (Trident Maple)	6 m (20 ft)	Red in autumn	Insignificant	Winged samara
Acer palmatum dwarf cultivars (Japanese Maple cultivars)	1–3 m (3–10 ft)	Dainty, colourful	Insignificant	Winged samara
Albizia distachya (Cape Wattle)	5–8 m (16–26 ft)	Feathery	Yellow	Legume
Albizia julibrissin (Silk Tree)	5–6 m (16–20 ft)	Ferny	White and pink	Legume
Arbutus unedo (Irish Strawberry Tree)	6 m (20 ft)	Dark green	White	Red, edible
Banksia marginata (Silver Banksia)	6 m (20 ft)	Silvery below	Greenish yellow	Erect cone
Cornus florida (Flowering Dogwood)	6 m (20 ft)	Autumn colours	White or greenish yellow	Small red berry
Dais cotinifolia (Pompon Tree)	5 m (16 ft)	Bright green	Mauve-pink	Insignificant
Dombeya tiliacea (Dombeya)	6 m (20 ft)	Dull dark green	White	Capsule
Eucalyptus lehmanni (Bushy Yate)	6 m (20 ft)	Dull green	Yellow green	Woody capsule
Eucalyptus perriniana (Spinning Gum)	7 m (23 ft)	Silvery juvenile leaves	White	Woody capsule
Eucalyptus torquata (Coral Gum)	7 m (23 ft)	Dull green	Coral red	Woody capsule
Fraxinus excelsior 'Aurea' (Golden Ash)	10 m (33 ft)	Lemon; gold in autumn	Insignificant	Insignificant
Hoheria populnea (New Zealand Lacebark)	5 m (16 ft)	Broad	White	Small nutlets
Homalanthus populifolius (Bleeding Heart Tree)	5 m (16 ft)	Green	Insignificant	Purple berry
Hymenosporum flavum (Native Frangipani)	8 m (26 ft)	Dark green, shiny	Yellow, fragrant	Woody capsule
Malus species (Crab Apple)	5 m (16 ft)	Dull green	Many colours	Small to medium apples
Melaleuca lanceolata (Black Paperbark)	7 m (23 ft)	Dull green-grey	White, cream	Woody capsule
Melia azedarach (White Cedar)	10 m (33 ft)	Dark green, shiny, feathery	Lavender-blue clusters	Orange berries
Pittosporum crassifolium (Karo)	6 m (20 ft)	Dark green, silver under	Dark red, perfumed	Black berries
Prunus cerasifera varieties (Flowering Cherry-plum)	8 m (26 ft)	Various colours	White or pink	Red or yellow, edible
Prunus subhirtella 'Pendula' (Weeping Cherry)	8 m (26 ft)	Green	Pink to white	Small cherry
Virgilia capensis (Cape Virgilia)	6 m (20 ft)	Light green, ferny	Pink to mauve, fragrant	Legume

BARK	SUITABLE CLIMATIC ZONES	REMARKS
Not outstanding feature	Cool humid; warm humid; very warm humid; hot dry	Good specimen tree; evergreen
Coarsely flaky	Cool humid; warm humid; hot dry; cold mountains and tablelands	Young shoots colour well; deciduous
Not outstanding feature	Cool humid; warm humid; hot dry; cold mountains and tablelands	Good foliage colours; attractive habit; excellent pot specimens
Not outstanding feature	Cool humid; warm humid; very warm humid	Flowers in close clusters resemble wattle
Not outstanding feature	Cool humid; warm humid; very warm humid; hot tropical coastal	Good shape; leaves like Jacaranda; deciduous
Grey when young; then red-brown	Cool humid; warm humid; very warm humid; hot dry; cold mountains and tablelands	Flowers resemble Lily-of-the-valley; evergreen
Not outstanding feature	Cool humid; warm humid; very warm humid	Withstands salt spray; evergreen
Squarish pattern on old bark	Cool humid; cold mountains and tablelands	Autumn colours red and orange; deciduous
Upper twigs olive green	Cool humid; warm humid; very warm humid; hot dry	Flowers massed; deciduous
Not outstanding feature	Cool humid; warm humid; very warm humid; hot dry	Some leaves colour in autumn; evergreen
Smooth, greyish brown	Cool humid; warm humid; hot dry; cold mountains and tablelands	Needs light, well-drained soil; resistant to salt spray; good screen
Smooth, blotched	Cool humid; warm humid; cold mountains and tablelands	Some juvenile foliage always present on adult tree
Rough, grey	Warm humid; very warm humid	Good tub plant; resists drought and frost
Orange-yellow twigs	Cool humid; warm humid; cold mountains and tablelands	Yellow twigs have distinctive black buds; deciduous
Netted bark	Cool humid; warm humid; hot dry; cold mountains and tablelands	Pretty variegated forms available; evergreen
Not outstanding feature	Cool humid; warm humid; very warm humid; hot tropical coastal; hot dry	Heart shaped leaves — some turn red
Not outstanding feature	Warm humid; very warm humid; hot tropical coastal; hot dry	Upright, open growth; evergreen
Not outstanding feature	Cool humid; warm humid; cold mountains and tablelands	Double-flowered sorts may not fruit; deciduous
Papery	Climate not critical	Stands heat, wet or lime soils; resists drought and frost
Brown with shallow vertical fissures	Cool humid; warm humid; very warm humid; hot dry	Frost tender when young; good screen or tub plant
Not outstanding feature	Cool humid; warm humid; very warm humid; hot dry; cold mountains and tablelands	Stands coastal position; resists drought and frost; evergreen
Dark brown	Cool humid; warm humid; hot dry; cold mountains and tablelands	Grown mainly for coloured leaves; deciduous
Dark brown	Cool humid; warm humid; hot dry; cold mountains and tablelands	Long, pendulous branches; several cultivars; deciduous
Not outstanding feature	Warm humid; very warm humid; hot tropical coastal	Prefers sandy soil; evergreen

For those gardeners with tiny backyards who require shrubs to become quickly established in order to lend a mature feeling to the landscape, see `Quick-growing shrubs for gardeners in a hurry', pages 86–7.

ABUTILON SPECIES
(CHINESE LANTERN)

Suitable for containers, cottage, formal and Mediterranean-style gardens; tolerates full sun to partial shade.

These attractive evergreen shrubs reach 3 m (10 ft) at maturity. Their pendulous bell-shaped flowers resemble Hibiscus. Of the many varieties of *Abutilon*, a few have variegated leaves.

The low-growing *A. megapotamicum* has a trailing habit and is useful as a groundcover or spillover from raised beds.

The *Abutilon* species is fast growing and easily maintained. Growing on only moderately rich soil and tip-pruning will ensure compact growth in small gardens.

BOUVARDIA SPECIES
(BOUVARDIA)

Suitable for containers, cottage and formal gardens; prefers full sun or partial shade.

These small shrubs grow to a height and spread of around 1 m (3 ft), and bear tubular flowers. The hybrids bear red, pink or white, single or double flowers. *B. humboldti* has fragrant white flowers from summer to autumn.

Bouvardias like a warm, sunny and sheltered spot. Too much shade will weaken their stems and result in fewer blooms. They are frost susceptible and happiest in warm temperate regions.

BRUNFELSIA BONODORA
(YESTERDAY-TODAY-TOMORROW)

Suitable for containers, cottage and formal gardens, hedges; prefers full sun or partial shade.

These rounded, evergreen shrubs reach 2–3 m (7–10 ft) in height. Fragrant flowers of different shades of purple occur at the same time on the shrub: blooms begin as a deep purple before turning to lavender and fading to white.

Brunfelsia is easily maintained and prefers a fertile loam and generous watering.

CAMELLIA SPECIES
(CAMELLIA)

Suitable for containers, cottage and formal gardens, hedges; prefers partial shade.

Camellias have glossy evergreen foliage, beautiful flowers, and reach a height of 2–5 m (7–16 ft). They are available in several sizes, in solid and variegated shades of pink, red and white, and in a variety of colour and form (singles, delicate semi-doubles and formal doubles).

C. sasanqua looks delicate, but it is a hardy and quick-growing species. Although naturally tall (to 3 m/10 ft) at maturity, it may be pruned to shape or espaliered on walls or fences to overcome space limitations at maturity. Flowers bloom from autumn to early winter.

C. japonica, more formal in appearance, has a flowering period from late autumn to early spring, depending on the variety. Miniature varieties are available.

C. reticulata has a more open habit, and its flowers are especially beautiful.

The *Camellia* species prefers a neutral to slightly acid soil.

CHOISYA TERNATA
(MEXICAN ORANGE BLOSSOM)

Suitable for containers, cottage, formal and Mediterranean-style gardens, hedges; prefers full sun or partial shade.

This attractive shrub grows to around 1 m (3 ft) in height and can be used as a specimen or hedging plant. The scented, white spring flowers resemble orange blossom. The leaves are glossy dark green and aromatic.

It is a very hardy shrub, preferring fertile, well-drained soil, but will grow in almost any soil or situation, including the seaside.

COLEONEMA PULCHRUM
(DIOSMA)

Suitable for formal gardens, hedges; prefers full sun.

Diosma has soft, aromatic foliage, and tiny pink flowers. It grows to 1.5 m (5 ft) but can be pruned to a lower hedge.

C. p. 'Sunset Gold' is a compact, dwarf form with a squat habit displaying golden foliage in sun-exposed positions. Treat informally, or clip to a rigid shape for a more formal situation.

DAPHNE SPECIES
(DAPHNE)

Suitable for containers, cottage, formal and Mediterranean-style gardens; prefers partial shade.

D. odora can reach 2 m (7 ft) high and wide, but generally grows to 1 m (3 ft). In winter and spring clusters of deep pink buds open to pale pink, fragrant flowers. *D. o.* 'Variegata' has leaves margined with cream, and *D. o.* 'Alba' has pure white flowers.

Daphne can be difficult to grow, requiring a sheltered position, filtered sunlight, an acid soil, and reliable drainage. It resents root disturbance.

DENDRANTHEMA FRUTESCENS
(MARGUERITE DAISY)

Suitable for containers, cottage, formal and Mediterranean-style gardens, hedges; prefers full sun.

These rounded, evergreen shrubs grow to 1 m (3 ft). The flowers are yellow, pink or white, with a yellow central disc. They can be grown in shrubberies, perennial borders or in pots or tubs. In a cottage garden they mix well with soft-wooded perennials.

They grow quickly, flower abundantly, and tolerate hot, dry conditions. Grow in an open sunny position with protection from strong winds. To discourage legginess, pick the flowers or cut back after flowering.

FELICIA AMELLOIDES
(BLUE DAISY)

Suitable for containers, cottage and Mediterranean-style gardens; prefers full sun or partial shade.

This small shrub grows to 45–50 cm (18–20 in) in height and is ideal for small gardens. The flowers are violet-blue with a yellow central disc and are most abundant during spring and summer. Blue Daisies are effective in perennial or shrub borders or as a massed display.

Constant tip-pruning ensures its tidy habit is maintained. *Felicia* is salt tolerant, fast growing, and easily maintained.

FUCHSIA HYBRIDS
(FUCHSIA)

Suitable for containers, cottage and formal gardens; prefers full or partial shade.

Being small in stature with a delicate habit, these make excellent additions to areas of dappled shade in small gardens. Some species lend themselves to standardising and many varieties are suitable for hanging baskets.

All species thrive in slightly acid, reasonably rich, moist, well-drained soil in tropical and temperate climates. Mulch to protect surface roots. Straggly growth can be avoided by tip-pruning.

GARDENIA SPECIES AND CULTIVARS
(GARDENIA)

Suitable for containers, cottage and formal gardens, hedges; prefers full sun or partial shade.

These shrubs bear exquisitely scented white flowers in early autumn and spring. The dark green leaves are very attractive, dense and shiny.

Gardenia augusta grows to 2 m (7 ft) and has medium-sized double flowers. The cultivars

'Professor Pucci' and 'Magnifica' have large flowers. *G. a.* 'Radicans' is a prostrate shrub, growing 30–45 cm (12–18 in.), with smaller leaves and flowers, a profuse habit, and is especially suitable for pots, petite gardens or low borders.

Gardenias prefer a sheltered, warm, sunny, temperate to subtropical climate, and an acid soil enriched with organic material.

In spring and summer, fertilise and water. The only pruning required is the picking of the flowers.

HEBE SPECIES AND CULTIVARS
(VERONICA)

Suitable for containers, formal and Mediterranean-style gardens, hedges; prefers full sun or partial shade.

Many species grow easily in an open, sunny position and are salt and wind tolerant. One of the best of the Hebes for areas subject to salt winds is *H.* × *franciscana* 'Blue Gem', which grows to 1–1.5 m (3–5 ft) and has deep violet flowers.

All Hebes are useful for providing a dense groundcover, for massing in a garden bed, or for trimming into a low, tight hedge.

Hebes are wind tolerant, fast growing and easily maintained, liking any well-drained soil.

HELIOTROPIUM ARBORESCENS
(CHERRY PIE)

Suitable for containers and cottage gardens; prefers full sun or partial shade.

This is a cottage garden favourite and suitable for a mixed shrubbery, or as a border plant or container specimen. It can grow 1.2 m (4 ft) tall and 1 m (3 ft) wide, and has fragrant, small, lilac flowers.

Two notable cultivars are 'Aureum', with variegated leaves and mauve flowers, and 'Lord Roberts', with dark purple flowers and deep purple-green leaves.

Heliotropium likes warm, well-drained soil and is happiest in warm-temperate to tropical

areas. It does not tolerate frost. To encourage a dense and bushy habit, prune back after flowering.

HIBISCUS
(HIBISCUS)

Suitable for containers, formal and Mediterranean-style gardens, hedges; prefers full sun.

Hybiscus hybrids are available in a variety of colours, including white and all shades of pink, purple, red or yellow. The large, trumpet-shaped flowers appear in summer and have prominent stamens. Shrubs vary in height.

'Crown of Warringah' (double, apricot), 'Miss Veno' (single, pink), 'Nathan Charles' (single, cerise), 'Powder Puff' (double, pale pink) and 'Surfrider' (single, orange with red centre) are among the wide selection of low growers.

Hibiscus rosa-sinensis hybrids tolerate salty winds quite well and are suitable for growing in coastal situations.

HYDRANGEA MACROPHYLLA
(HYDRANGEA)

Suitable for container, cottage and formal gardens; prefers full or partial shade.

Hydrangea macrophylla is the common Hydrangea grown in so many gardens. It is the parent of Hortensias (large globe-shaped flower clusters) and Lacecaps (a ring of flowers surrounding a hump of smaller flowers).

Both types have hybrids of varying habits, and selections should be made according to foliage and flower preference in addition to the hybrid's ultimate height and habit relative to the amount of space available.

Hydrangeas bloom in summer, and have pink, violet, blue or white flowers. Acid soil supports blue flowers, and alkaline soil, pink. White flowers remain white.

Hydrangeas grow equally well in the ground or in pots and tubs (where it is often easier to control flower colour). They enjoy sun for limited periods, especially early morning, but are at their best in the light shade. In the garden, they are an excellent addition to shrubberies, shaded borders or planted in a group.

The Lacecaps are a very effective feature plant or can be used as an accent amongst herbaceous and soft-wooded perennials.

LANTANA HYBRIDS
(LANTANA)

Suitable for containers and Mediterranean-style gardens, hedges; prefers full sun.

The hybrids are a better choice than the species, especially for warm coastal regions, as the species is likely to become a rampant weed. Excellent *Lantana camara* hybrids for the small garden include 'Drap d'Or', a dwarf variety with golden-yellow flowers; 'Gol Gol', which grows to 1 m (3 ft) and has copper-yellow flowers darkening to red; and 'Snowflake', which has white flowers. 'Christine' is a prostrate hybrid, grows to 50 cm (20 in.), and has orange-red flowers. All can be pruned to form a neat hedge.

L. montevidensis is a trailing species with lilac flowers. It will trail down a wall or fence, or cascade from hanging baskets or pots. It flowers all year.

Lantanas like a sunny position, are evergreen, and will flower for most of the year. These hardy plants require little attention and will tolerate harsh coastal conditions.

LAVANDULA SPECIES
(LAVENDER)

Suitable for containers, cottage, formal and Mediterranean-style gardens, hedges; prefers full sun.

The highly scented *L. angustifolia* (English Lavender) grows to 1.5 m (5 ft). It has narrow pale grey-green leaves, and spikes of purple flowers appear in summer. Flowers in white or other shades of purple are available.

L. dentata (French Lavender) grows to 1.5 m

(5 ft). It has small grey-green leaves, and its spikes of slightly perfumed lavender-blue flowers appear from winter through to summer.

L. stoechas (Italian Lavender) grows to 1 m (3 ft). It has narrow leaves, and spikes of deep purple flowers appear in spring and summer.

MICHELIA FIGO
(PORT WINE MAGNOLIA)

Suitable for containers, formal gardens, hedges; prefers full sun or partial shade.

This erect, rounded shrub grows to 3 m (10 ft) and has lustrous foliage, densely packed — making it an ideal privacy screening plant in smallish town gardens. The scent of the rather insignificant flowers is added bonus. *Michelia figo* can be treated as a specimen in the formal garden and takes kindly to being confined to a large pot or tub.

MURRAYA PANICULATA
(ORANGE JESSAMINE)

Suitable for containers, formal and Mediterranean-style gardens, hedges; prefers full sun or partial shade.

This sweetly scented evergreen shrub grows to 3 m (10 ft), makes a useful windbreak or hedge, and gives shelter and shade to smaller plants. It has star-shaped flowers, similar to orange blossoms, and deep green glossy leaves.

It prefers a tropical to mild temperate climate. A light trimming after flowering is required.

PHILADELPHUS SPECIES
(MOCK ORANGE)

Suitable for container, cottage and formal gardens; prefers full sun or partial shade.

These elegant deciduous shrubs have fragrant white clusters of single or double flowers in early summer.

The well-known hybrid 'Virginal' grows to 3 m (10 ft), and may be deemed too large for a very small garden with its arching canes forming a broadish crown. In such cases choose from the smaller species: *P. microphyllus* (Small-leafed Mock Orange), which grows to 1 m (3 ft), or *P.* 'Corquette'.

Any reasonable garden soil will support these hardy shrubs. They like a sunny, sheltered position in most climates except hot tropical and dry inland areas.

PLUMBAGO AURICULATA
(LEADWORT)

Suitable for cottage and Mediterranean-style gardens, hedges; prefers full sun.

This semi-climbing shrub makes an attractive plant for hedges or shrubberies. It has light green leaves, and in late summer through to autumn is covered with pale blue flowers. 'Alba' is a white-flowering variety.

It requires a late-winter trim to maintain its shape or, in small gardens, a hard prune to control its vigorous growth. It thrives in temperate to tropical climates, and resists heat and drought conditions in sunny, frost-free areas.

RHODODENDRON
(AZALEA)

Suitable for containers, cottage and formal gardens; prefers full or partial shade.

Azaleas are popular shrubs, delivering a spectacular show mainly in spring and spot flowering at other times of the year.

The Gumpo, Kurume and many of the Belgian hybrids are particularly suited to small gardens, as they are of compact habit.

Popular azaleas include the following: Addy Wery (Kurume, vermilion flowers); Blaauw's Pink (dwarf, salmon pink), California Peach (Belgian hybrid, peach pink), Christmas Cheer (Kurume, crimson), Comtesse de Kerchove (Belgian hybrid, pale salmon), Elsa Karga (Belgian hybrid, copper red), Esemerelda (Kurume, pale pink), Fairy Queen (Kurume, apple-blossom pink), Gumpo Stripe (dwarf, white with mauve-red stripes), Kirin (Kurume,

pink), Leopold Astrid (Belgian hybrid, white with rose margin), Martha Gardener (Belgian hybrid, dark red), Peach Blossom (Kurume, rosy lavender-pink), Penelope (Kurume, white with lavender edge), Pink Cloud (Kurume, light pink), Red Wings (hybrid, rosy red), Snowdrift (Belgian hybrid, white), Snowflake (Kurume, white), and Sweet Sixteen (Belgian hybrid, pink with frilled edge).

Azaleas require minimal space for their shallow root system, and are therefore ideal for pots and tubs. For unity of design, two or three plants massed and restricted to one colour are most effective.

RONDELETIA SPECIES
(RONDELETIA)

Suitable for containers and formal gardens, hedges; prefers full sun or partial shade.

These elegant shrubs have bell-shaped flowers and broad, light green, oval leaves.

R. amoena is a large shrub, growing to 2.5 m (8 ft). Its rounded heads of perfumed flowers, in salmon-pink with yellow throats, appear in spring.

R. odorata grows to 1.5 m (5 ft), and has fragrant orange-red summer flowers with a yellow throat.

R. strigosa grows to 1.5 m (5 ft), and has long, arching canes suitable for espalier treatment. Its bright crimson flowers appear in spring and summer.

Shrubs in the *Rondeletia* species are suitable for average soil, and will tolerate the coast in warm temperate areas.

ROSMARINUS SPECIES
(ROSEMARY)

Suitable for containers and Mediterranean-style gardens, hedges; prefers full sun.

R. officinalis grows to a height and width of 1.5 m (5 ft) and is suitable for an evergreen hedge or a border shrub.

R. lavandulaceus makes a useful groundcover or a pretty container plant. It is especially effective trailing over a bank or wall.

Rosemary's small, pale blue or white flowers appear in spring and summer; its aromatic leaves are narrow, stiff and leathery with a prominent centre vein.

Rosemary is native to the northern Mediterranean coastline and does best in areas with a dry, temperate climate and average, well-drained soil.

SPIRAEA SPECIES
(MAY BUSH)

Suitable for cottage and formal gardens, hedges; prefers full sun or partial shade.

S. cantoniensis is a graceful, deciduous shrub suitable for an informal hedge. It has slender, arching canes. Dense clusters of white flowers appear in spring. Growing to a rounded shrub of 2.5 m (8 ft), it can be accommodated in city gardens with reasonable space. Prune after flowering, removing older canes at ground level — pruning in any other fashion will destroy the graceful shape of the bush.

For gardens of pocket-handkerchief size a more suitable choice would be *S. × bumalda* 'Antony Waterer', a charming small shrub bearing small bright crimson flowers in dense heads throughout summer. Naturally dainty of habit, prune only to shape, if necessary.

VIBURNUM TINUS
(VIBURNUM)

Suitable for containers, formal and Mediterranean-style gardens, hedges; tolerates full sun to partial shade.

Viburnum tinus grows to 3 m (10 ft) high and 2 m (7 ft) wide, and makes an excellent hedge. The flowers are faintly perfumed and pinkish white, appearing in autumn and winter. The leaves are dark green and shiny.

Viburnum is a hardy shrub, and will grow in coastal areas.

HEDGING PLANTS

- *Brunfelsia bonodora* (Yesterday-Today-Tomorow)
- *Buxus sempervirens* (Common Box)
- *Camellia* species
- *Choisya ternata* (Mexican Orange Blossom)
- *Clivea miniata* (Kaffir Lily)
- *Coleonema pulchrum* (Diosma)
- *Dendrathema frutescens* (Marguerite Daisy)
- *Gardenia* species and cultivars
- *Gazania* hybrids
- *Hebe* species and cultivars (Veronica)
- *Hibiscus*
- *Lantana* hybrids
- *Laurus nobilis* (Bay Tree)
- *Lavandula* (Lavender)
- *Lonicera nitida* (Box-leafed Honeysuckle)
- *Michelia figo* (Port Wine Magnolia)
- *Murraya paniculata* (Orange Jessamine)
- *Plumbago auriculata* (Leadwort)
- *Rondeletia* (Rondeletia)
- *Rosmarinus* (Rosemary)
- *Spiraea* (May Bush)
- *Viburnum tinus* (Viburnum)

QUICK-GROWING SHRUBS FOR GARDENERS IN A HURRY

NAME OF SHRUB	HEIGHT	LEAVES	FLOWERS	
Abelia species (Abelia)	2 m (7 ft)	Glossy	White, pink bells	
Abutilon megapotamicum (Brazilian Bell Flower)	0.5 m (1½ ft)	Variegated green and yellow	Red and yellow	
Acacia myritofolia (Myrtle Wattle)	2 m (7 ft)	Dark green	Pale yellow	
Boronia denticulata (Mauve Boronia)	1 m (3 ft)	Fine toothed	Small clusters, mauve-pink	
Callistemon 'Captain Cook' (Captain Cook Bottlebrush)	2 m (7 ft)	Green	Bright red	
Cistus species (Rock Rose)	1–2 m (3–7 ft)	Dark green	Open flowers, many colours	
Cytisus species (Flowering Broom)	2–3 m (7–10 ft)	Almost leafless	Many colour types	
Eranthemum pulchellum (Blue Sage)	1 m (3 ft)	Handsome, heavily veined	Blue and lilac	
Escallonia species (Escallonia)	2–4 m (7–13 ft)	Some species glossy	White, pink or red	
Grevillea lavandulacea (Lavender Grevillea)	2 m (7 ft)	Silvery grey	Pink	
Hibiscus rosa-sinensis (Hibiscus)	2–3 m (7–10 ft)	Dark green, glossy	Large flowers, many colours	
Lantana montevidensis (Trailing Lantana)	1–1.5 m (3–5 ft)	Small, slightly hairy	Mauve, white	
Melaleuca fulgens (Scarlet Honey Myrtle)	2 m (7 ft)	Grey-green	Red or deep pink	
Nerium oleander varieties (Oleander)	2–3 m (7–10 ft)	Dark green, glossy	White, pink, salmon, red	
Plumbago auriculata (Plumbago)	2 m (7 ft)	Dull green	Pale blue or white	
Prostanthera rotundifolia (Round Leaf Mintbush)	3 m (10 ft)	Small, deep green	Masses, deep blue to purple	
Tecomaria capensis (Cape Honeysuckle)	3 m (10 ft)	Deep green, glossy	Bright orange-red	
Viburnum tinus (Viburnum)	3 m (10 ft)	Dark green, leathery	Clusters, white tinged pink	
Westringia fruticosa (Westringia)	2 m (7 ft)	Greyish to bluish grey	White to pale mauve	

SUITABLE CLIMATIC ZONES	REMARKS
Cool humid; warm humid; very warm humid; hot tropical coastal; dry inland; hot dry; temperate mountains and tablelands	Arching branches; tolerates wind
Cool humid; warm humid; very warm humid; hot tropical coastal; hot dry	Prostrate, spreads to 2 m (7 ft); pinch back leaves to improve flowering
Climate not critical	Prune each year after flowering; resists drought and frost
Cool humid; warm humid; hot dry	Good drainage necessary; frost tender
Cool humid; warm humid; very warm humid; hot tropical coastal; hot dry	Dwarf plant, weeping habit
Cool humid; warm humid; very warm humid; hot tropical coastal; dry inland; hot dry; temperate mountains and tablelands	Petals with papery texture; suits Mediterranean-style gardens
Cool humid; warm humid; hot dry; cold mountains and tablelands	Some flowers are bi-coloured
Warm humid; very warm humid; hot tropical coastal	Good container plant; drought and frost tender
Cool humid; warm humid; hot dry; cold mountains and tablelands	Many attractive cultivars
Cool humid; warm humid; very warm humid; hot dry	Will spread wide to 3 m (10 ft); resists drought and frost
Warm humid; very warm humid; hot tropical coastal	Cut back late winter; tolerates salt
Cool humid; warm humid; very warm humid; hot tropical coastal; dry inland; hot dry	Good spillover plant; tolerates wind
Cool humid; warm humid; hot dry	Needs good drainage; resists drought and frost
Cool humid; warm humid; very warm humid; hot tropical coastal; dry inland; hot dry; temperate mountains and tablelands; warm mountains and tablelands	Variegated sort available; tolerates salt wind
Warm humid; very warm humid; hot tropical coastal	Suckers freely from base; prune to shape annually
Cool humid; warm humid; hot dry; temperate mountains and tablelands	Prune to shape after flowering; resists drought and frost
Cool humid; warm humid; very warm humid; hot tropical coastal	Yellow and orange species also
Cool humid; warm humid; very warm humid; hot dry; cold mountains and tablelands	Withstands clipping; good hedging plant
Cool humid; warm humid; very warm humid; hot dry	Needs good drainage; tolerates salt and wind

AJUGA REPTANS
(BLUE BUGLE)

Suitable for containers, cottage, formal and Mediterranean-style gardens; prefers full or partial shade.

Ajuga reptans is a fast spreading and hardy carpeting plant for a shaded position. It is especially suitable for hard-to-cover areas beneath established trees. The leaves are very attractive, and the tall flower spikes appear in spring. The species has dark green leaves and blue-purple flowers.

'Alba' has white flowers; 'Glacier' has variegated green and cream leaves; 'Burgundy Lace' has variegated cream and maroon leaves; 'Multicolor' has variegated pink, burgundy and cream leaves and blue flowers; 'Jungle Beauty' has large green leaves and long flower spikes.

AQUILEGIA VULGARIS
(GRANNY'S BONNETS, OR COLUMBINE)

Suitable for containers, cottage and formal gardens; prefers full sun or partial shade.

Bonnet-shaped spurred blooms appear in spring, in colours of blue, purple, rose, yellow, cream or white. The large clover-like leaves are blue-green above and grey beneath. Many strains are available, including mini hybrids.

ASTER NOVI-BELGII
(PERENNIAL ASTER)

Suitable for containers, cottage and formal gardens; prefers full sun.

The flowers of this hardy, fast-growing perennial appear year-round, but mainly in late summer and early autumn, in white, pink, mauve, blue or purple with a red or yellow centre. It is a useful plant for accents and also for a massed display. Heights range from 45 to 150 cm (1½ to 5 ft).

Select dwarf types for a carpeting effect or for massing in small spaces.

AURINIA SAXATILIS
(YELLOW ALYSSUM)

Suitable for container, cottage, formal and Mediterranean-style gardens; prefers full sun.

Flat-topped clusters of small, yellow flowers appear in spring. The leaves are hairy and grey-green. It is a spreading plant, suitable for accent bedding or a wall garden, and can grow to 25 cm (10 in.).

BERGENIA CORDIFOLIA
(SAXIFRAGA)

Suitable for containers, cottage, formal and Mediterranean-style gardens; prefers full or partial shade.

Saxifraga grows to 30 cm (1 ft). Clusters of pink, single flowers on short, thick stems, appear in winter and early spring. The leaves are green, rounded, large and glossy.

Saxifraga is a low-maintenance plant and is especially useful for areas of dappled shade. It would not suit tropical or dry climates.

BRACHYCOME SPECIES

Suitable for containers, cottage, formal and Mediterranean-style gardens; prefers full sun.

Many species of perennial *Brachycome* are available, with daisy-like flowers in blue, white, pink, and purple appearing from spring to late summer. Heights vary from 30–60 cm (1–2 ft), according to species.

They are suitable for hanging baskets or pots, and also make an excellent groundcover for a well-drained, open position.

(The summer-flowering *B. iberidifloa* (Swan River Daisy) is a self-reproducing annual.)

CERASTIUM TOMENTOSUM
(SNOW IN SUMMER)

Suitable for containers, cottage, formal and Mediterranean-style gardens; prefers full sun.

This plant grows to 7.5 cm (3 in.) high and 30 cm (12 in.) wide. It has soft, silver-grey leaves. White flowers appear from spring to mid-summer. It makes an excellent plant for foliage contrast, and its spreading habit makes it suitable for open, well-drained areas.

CLIVIA MINIATA
(KAFFIR LILY, OR CLIVIA)

Suitable for containers, formal and Mediterranean-style gardens; prefers full or partial shade.

Clivia is clump-forming hardy perennial with dark green strap-like leaves, and grows to 45 cm (18 in.) high. Clusters of up to 20 orange tubular flowers appear atop the stems in late winter to early spring. (White- and red-flowering varieties are scarce.) In small gardens they can be planted uniformly as borders or low hedges, grouped in clumps in perennial beds, or potted up as tub specimens.

CONVOLVULUS MAURITANICUS
(GROUND MORNING GLORY)

Suitable for containers, cottage, formal and Mediterranean-style gardens; prefers full sun or partial shade.

This hardy and quick-growing perennial grows to a height of 15 cm (6 in.) and a spread of 1 m (3 ft), and bears lavender-blue flowers from spring to autumn. It is suitable as a groundcover or as a trailing plant from raised beds, pots or hanging baskets.

DENDRANTHEMA MAXIMA
(SHASTA DAISY)

Suitable for containers, cottage, formal and Mediterranean-style gardens; prefers full sun.

This mid-height perennial has large white flowers with golden centres in summer. It is suitable for bedding, borders or pots. Other varieties have double flowers or fringed petals.

ERIGERON SPECIES
(FLEABANE)

Suitable for containers, cottage, formal and Mediterranean-style gardens; prefers full sun or partial shade.

This low-growing perennial bears masses of small white daisies from spring to autumn, and throughout the year in warm climates. Heights vary from 30 to 50 cm (12 to 20 in.). It will quickly spread to 50 cm (20 in.) as a groundcover or along a border, and can be used to fill garden pockets.

GAZANIA HYBRIDS
(GAZANIA)

Suitable for containers and Mediterranean-style gardens, hedges; prefers full sun.

These daisy-flowered perennials grow to 30 cm (12 in.) high and form dense tufts, spreading to 50 cm (20 in.) wide. They have large, showy daisy-like summer flowers with cream, yellow, orange, red and pink petals, and black or yellow centres. Varieties with two-toned petals are available.

Gazanias are suitable for a bed or border, and will grow in poor soil in dry conditions.

GERBERA JAMESONII
(GERBERA, OR TRANSVAAL DAISY)

Suitable for containers, cottage and formal gardens; prefers full sun.

A beautiful and useful perennial, blooming from spring to autumn. It grows to a height of 30 cm (12 in.). The daisy-like flowers are red-orange; white hybrids are available, as are shades of yellow, orange, red and violet. The flowers occur on long stems and last well in the garden or in a vase.

It likes sandy loam, regular watering, good drainage, and some fertiliser.

HELLEBORUS ORIENTALIS
(LENTEN ROSE, OR HELLEBORE)

Suitable for containers, cottage and formal gardens; prefers full or partial shade.

This perennial grows to about 30 cm (1 ft) high. The flowers of this perennial are somewhat like a five-petalled rose in appearance, and are creamy white with a rosy-purple tinge. Flowers appear in winter and spring. *Helleborus* looks especially effective planted in clumps.

Hybrids are available in shades of purple, rose and plum as well as white.

Helleborus likes moist, rich soil and is easily maintained.

HEMEROCALLIS CULTIVARS
(DAY LILY)

Suitable for containers, cottage and Mediterranean-style gardens; prefers full sun.

The individual flowers last only a day but each stem carries many, separately blooming, flowers.

These clump-forming perennials grow to around 1.2 m (4 ft) high and are suitable for mass planting or accents, or in shrubberies or borders or accent plants. They can be incorporated into shrubberies. Many varieties are available, in many colours.

They are hardy, fast growing and easily maintained.

PLATYCODON GRANDIFLORUS
(BALLOON FLOWER)

Suitable for containers, cottage and formal gardens; prefers full sun or partial shade.

This pretty perennial grows to 60 cm (2 ft). Its balloon-shaped buds open to bell-shaped purple flowers in summer. It is useful for edging paths or beds, or as a spillover plant for raised beds. 'Misato Dwarf' grows to 50 cm (20 in.) and is especially suited to tiny gardens.

POLEMONIUM PULCHERRIMUM
(JACOB'S LADDER)

Suitable for containers, cottage and formal gardens; prefers full sun or partial shade.

P. p. 'Blue Dove' is a dainty perennial clumping to 25 cm (10 in.). It has fresh, ferny leaves and sprays of lavender, cup-shaped flowers. It blooms from spring to early autumn but peaks in summer.

Plant several for a border or use in the front row of perennial plantings.

PRIMULA × POLYANTHA
(POLYANTHUS)

Suitable for containers, cottage, formal and Mediterranean-style gardens; prefers full or partial shade.

This perennial is a cross between the old polyanthus and the English primrose. Growing 15–25 cm (6–10 in.) tall, it is ideal for borders in city gardens. Polyanthus is available in a range of colours, including blues, reds, pinks and yellows.

If plants are purchased when they are flowering they can either be used as temporary indoor plants or planted out to give the garden an immediate boost.

Polyanthus requires regular watering during dry spells, and will grow in most climates.

RHODANTHE ANTHEMOIDES
(SYN. *HELIPTERUM ANTHEMOIDES*) (PAPER DAISY)

Suitable for containers, cottage and formal gardens; prefers full sun or partial shade.

This perennial grows to a height of 40 cm (16 in.) and to a spread of 50 cm (20 in.). It has an erect stem and narrow leaves, and in summer bears white flowers with papery petals and a yellow centre.

It is suitable for pots, baskets, raised beds, pockets and borders.

SILENE MARITIMA
(WITCH'S THIMBLE)

Suitable for cottage and formal gardens; prefers full sun or partial shade.

This perennial grows to 30 cm (1 ft) and has white trumpet-shaped flowers in spring and pale blue-grey leaves. It is ideal as a groundcover for raised beds, rockeries and borders.

VIOLA SPECIES
(VIOLET)

Suitable for containers, cottage, formal and Mediterranean-style gardens; tolerates full sun to partial shade.

For shade or filtered sun areas, spreading clumps of *Viola odorata* (Sweet Violet) are beautiful. The large heart-shaped leaves are present all year, and the sweetly scented purple flowers appear in early spring. Cultivars are available in white, cream, pink and mauve, with single or double blooms. *V. odorata* will grow in temperate climate zones but produces more flowers in cooler areas.

V. hederacea (Native Violet) has scentless purple and white flowers. This clumping perennial will flourish in full sun or part shade.

GROUNDCOVERING PLANTS

- *Ajuga reptans* (Blue Bugle)
- *Ajuga reptans* 'Alba' (Carpet Bugle)
- *Anthemis* (Chamomile)
- *Arabis caucasica* 'Flore Pleno' (Double Rock Cress)
- *Armeria maritima* (Sea Pink, or Thrift)
- *Bergenia cordifolia* (Saxifraga)
- *Campanula portenschlagiana* (Bellflower)
- *Cerastium tomentosum* (Snow in Summer)
- *Convolvulus mauritanicus* (Ground Morning Glory)
- *Cotula dioica* (Cotula)
- *Cotula pulchella* (Brass Buttons)
- *Dampiera diversifolia* (Dampiera)
- *Dichondra repans* (Dichondra)
- *Erigeron* (Fleabane)
- *Fragaria chiloensis* (Wild Strawberry)
- *Frankenia laevis* (Sea Heath)
- *Gazania* hybrids
- *Geranium sanguineum* (Crane's Bill)
- *Heliotropium aborescens* (Cherry Pie)
- *Heterocentron elegans* (Spanish Shawl)
- *Hibbertia serphyllifolia* (Guinea Flower)
- *Houstonia caerulea* (Blue Cushion)
- *Lobularia maritima* (Alyssum)
- *Mentha pulegium* (Pennyroyal)
- *Mentha requienii* (Corsican Mint)
- *Myosotis sylvatica* (Forget-me-not)
- *Ophiopogon jaburan* (White Mondo Grass)
- *Ophiopogon japonicus* (Mondo Grass)
- *Pelargonium peltatum* (Ivy Geranium)
- *Phyla nodiflora* (Lippia)
- *Polygonum capitatum* (Knotweed)
- *Potentilla tabernaemontani* (Spring Cinquefoil)
- *Prunella* (Prunella)
- *Silene maritima* (Witch's Thimble)
- *Soleriolia soleirolii* (Angel's Tears)
- *Stachys byzantina* (Lamb's Ears)
- *Thymus* (Thyme)
- *Tropaeoleum majus* (Nasturtium)
- *Veronica prostrata* (Speedwell)
- *Viola hederacea* (Native Violet)
- *Viola odorata* (Sweet Violet)

Very few annuals need be eliminated from tiny gardens, as most are either small in stature or easily confined to a limited space.

As annuals have a one-year life cycle and are pulled out annually, they do not become invasive, although some will self-seed.

Annuals are useful for planting in newly established small gardens, filling out space until the framework of trees and shrubs gains height and substance.

Their quick growth provides some softening foliage and floral colour within a short period of time.

For almost immediate results, annuals can be purchased as advanced 'bloomers' or 'potted colour'.

AGERATUM HOUSTONIANUM
(FLOSS FLOWER)

Suitable for containers, cottage, formal and Mediterranean-style gardens; prefers full sun.

This hardy annual has mauve clusters of fluffy flowers, and grows to 40 cm (16 in.). Flowers occur all year, but mostly in summer.

Small cultivars that grow to 25 cm (10 in.) include 'Spindrift' and 'White Angel', both with white flowers, and 'Blue Mink', 'Blue Blazer' and 'Imperial Dwarf Blue'. The small cultivars suit massed planting in borders and being mixed with other plants in rockeries.

ALCEA ROSEA
(HOLLYHOCK)

Suitable for cottage gardens; prefers full sun or partial shade.

This hardy biennial grows to 2.5 m (8 ft) and has rounded heart-shaped leaves and bell-like flowers in red, pink, purple or white that appear in summer. 'Indian Spring' is an annual variety that has large semi-double flowers. Hollyhocks need to be protected from the wind, and are suitable for growing in clumps and as a background to small annuals.

ANTIRRHINUM MAJUS
(SNAPDRAGON)

Suitable for containers, cottage and Mediterranean-style gardens; prefers full sun.

Snapdragons have tubular double-lipped flowers in white and shades of yellow, orange, red, pink and purple; some varieties are bi-coloured. Four heights are available: tall, which grows to 75 cm (30 in.); medium, which grows to 50 cm (20 in.); semi-dwarf, which grows to 30 cm (12 in.); and dwarf, which grows to 25 cm (10 in.).

These old-fashioned flowers are suitable for bedding, containers and massed displays. Small varieties suitable for edgings and borders include 'Tom Thumb', 'Camelot' and the semi-dwarf 'Majestic'.

If the plants are cut back hard after their first flowering in autumn, then fertilised, they will flower again in spring.

BELLIS PERENNIS
(ENGLISH DAISY)

Suitable for containers, cottage and gardens; prefers full sun or partial shade.

These spring-flowering plants are especially suited to containers, borders and edgings. They grow to 10 cm (4 in.). If planted close together they will provide a massed display. They are available in white, red or pink.

CALLISTEPHUS CHINENSIS
(CHINA ASTER)

Suitable for containers and cottage gardens; prefers full sun or partial shade.

Many varieties are available, from dwarf bedding types to giants. The flowers are daisy-like, appear in summer and autumn, and are available in single or double forms in white and brilliant shades of pink and mauve. Their leaves are oval-shaped and bright green.

For a bedding display, a wilt-resistant variety (such as 'Giant Crego', 'American Beauty', 'California Giant' or 'King Mixed') would be the best choice.

CAMPANULA MEDIUM
(CANTERBURY BELL)

Suitable for cottage gardens; prefers full or partial shade.

Bell-shaped flowers in white, pink or lilac bloom from spring to early summer. They look very attractive planted behind small borders, and grow 45–60 cm (1½–2 ft).

CENTAUREA CYANUS
(CORNFLOWER)

Suitable for cottage gardens; prefers full sun.

Cornflowers are especially effective for drift planting in perennial borders. They bloom in spring. Apart from the well-known blue, cultivars are available in red, maroon, mauve, pink and white, and in dwarf varieties.

CHEIRANTHUS CHEIRI
(WALLFLOWER)

Suitable for cottage gardens; prefers full sun.

These sweetly scented, old-fashioned flowers are very popular for cottage gardens. The yellow, orange, pink and brown flowers appear in spring and early summer. Wallflowers are available in two heights: 25 cm (10 in.) and 60 cm (2 ft). They look very attractive in borders or as a bedding plant.

CLEOME HASSLERIANA
(SPIDER FLOWER)

Suitable for cottage gardens; prefers full sun or partial shade.

This tall, summer-flowering annual has pink, white or mauve flowers and very long stamens. The plants grow rapidly, to a height of 1.5 m (5 ft), and will disguise a fence effectively. They are also very suitable as a background in a garden bed, and do best in a mild to warm temperate climate.

COSMOS BIPINNATUS
(COSMOS)

Suitable for cottage and Mediterranean-style gardens; prefers full sun or partial shade.

Cosmos is available in single, semi-double, double and crested varieties, in pink, crimson, orange and white.

Tall (1–2 m/3–7 ft) varieties of this summer-flowering annual provide an attractive background in a garden bed. For shorter, more compact strains, consider the 'Ladybird' series (30 cm/1 ft) or 'Sonata' series (to 50 cm/18 in.).

It grows easily but is not frost-resistant, and has a tendency to self-seed.

DIANTHUS SPECIES
(PINK AND SWEET WILLIAM)

Suitable for containers, cottage, formal and Mediterranean-style gardens; prefers full sun or partial shade.

D. chinensis (Pink) has fragrant flowers in white, pink, red or mauve, in singles and doubles, often with lacy petals. Heights vary from 15 cm (6 in.) to 45 cm (18 in.). Pinks are effective in borders or as a groundcover in tiny gardens.

D. barbatus (Sweet William) blooms in spring and early summer, and grows 30–60 cm (1–2 ft). It is available in mixed and separate colourings of red, pink, maroon and mauve, and often has white markings. It is especially suited to pots, borders and beds.

DIGITALIS PURPUREA
(FOXGLOVE)

Suitable for containers, cottage and formal gardens; prefers full or partial shade.

These tall, erect biennials have closely packed spikes of long, tubular flowers in white, cream, purple or pink. They are suitable for mixed bedding displays and perennial borders. Strains are available in other colours and with flowers all around the stem.

Although tall (to 150 cm/5 ft), they do not take up much ground space, making them ideal candidates for the background of beds or for accent planting in confined spaces. Shorter strains include 'Foxy' (to 120 cm/4 ft) and 'Rapture' (to 35 cm/14 in.).

ESCHSCHOLZIA CALIFORNICA
(CALIFORNIAN POPPY)

Suitable for containers, cottage and Mediterranean-style gardens; prefers full sun.

This summer-flowering annual has finely cut leaves and brilliantly coloured, saucer-shaped blooms. It is hardy, preferring a sandy soil in a sunny location, and grows 30–45 cm (12–18 in.).

'Lemon Drops', low growing with miniature flowers resembling yellow tulips, is well-suited to pot culture.

GOMPHRENA GLOBOSA
(BACHELOR'S BUTTONS)

Suitable for containers, cottage and formal gardens; prefers full sun.

This compact summer-flowering annual grows to 30–45 cm (12–18 in.), and has stiff-petalled clover-like blooms in magenta, lavender, pink or white.

Dwarf varieties in the 'Buddy' series grow 20–30 cm (8–12 in.), and are suitable for an annual border, bedding or edging.

HELIANTHUS SPECIES
(SUNFLOWER)

Suitable for cottage gardens; prefers full sun.

The most widely cultivated annual type for home gardens, and very popular as a cut flower for indoor arrangements, is *H. decapetalus*. Medium sized, growing 1–1.5 m (3–5 ft), it is used for background or accent planting. A smaller type, suitable for a border plant, grows to 40 cm (16 in.).

Sunflowers bloom in summer, and need an open position, rich soil and abundant moisture.

LATHYRUS ODORATUS
(SWEET PEA)

Suitable for containers, cottage and formal gardens; prefers full sun.

This pretty, scented climber grows quickly and will cover a fence or trellis to a height of 2.5 m (8 ft). Flowers appear from late winter to early summer, and are available in a huge range of colours, including red, pink, mauve, purple, blue, white cream. Removing the spent blooms from the vine will lengthen the flowering period.

Dwarf strains, growing from 25 to 60 cm (10 in. to 2 ft), are ideal for borders, window boxes, raised beds, rockeries. 'Bijou', for example, grows to 45 cm (18 in.) and looks very pretty trailing from a container.

LOBELIA ERINUS
(EDGING LOBELIA)

Suitable for containers, cottage, formal and Mediterranean-style gardens; prefers full sun or partial shade.

This spring-flowering annual grows from 10 to 25 cm (4 to 10 in.) in height and is very useful for edgings, borders, raised beds, hanging baskets and window boxes.

Many cultivars are available. 'Crystal Palace' grows to 15 cm (6 in.), and has rich blue flowers and bronze-green leaves. 'String of Pearls' also grows to 15 cm (6 in.), and is a mixed punnet with a blend of pink, mauve, rosy purple, white and blue.

'Sapphire' grows to 25 cm (10 in.) and has blue flowers with a white 'eye'; its pendulous habit makes it very suitable for hanging baskets. Other cultivars with trailing stems include 'Fountain' and 'Basket Lobelia'.

LOBULARIA MARITIMA
(ALYSSUM, OR SWEET ALICE)

Suitable for containers, cottage, formal and Mediterranean-style gardens; prefers full sun or partial shade.

This hardy small plant flowers throughout the year in most climates and is indispensable for adding a softening effect to borders, path edges, garden beds or spaces between brick or stone pavers. It is also used as a carpeting or rock-wall plant and suits window boxes, planters and pots (including pots with potted bulbs).

Alyssum grows 7–25 cm (3–10 in.) tall and has spreading stems. It has tiny, green leaves and dense clusters of tiny white, pink, mauve or purple flowers. Cultivars include 'Carpet of Snow', which has pure white flowers and grows to 10 cm (4 in.), and 'Royal Carpet', which has deep violet flowers and grows to 10 cm (4 in.).

MATTHIOLA INCANA VAR. ANNUA
(STOCK)

Suitable for containers and cottage gardens; prefers full sun.

Stock has a heady, clove-like perfume. This popular spring-flowering annual comes in single and double forms, with white, cream, yellow, pink, lilac, red, deep crimson or purple flowers. Stock blooms from late winter to early summer, according to variety.

A range of heights and varieties are available, such as 'Giant Imperial', 'Giant Column' (50–75 cm/20–30 in.), 'Austral' (50 cm/20 in.), 'Dwarf Double' (25 cm/10 in.), and the dwarf 'Cinderella' series.

Remove spent blooms from the plant to lengthen the flowering period.

PAPAVER NUDICAULE
(ICELAND POPPY)

Suitable for containers, cottage and formal gardens; prefers full sun.

This magnificent plant grows to 60 cm (2 ft) and blooms from late winter into spring. It is suitable as a bedding plant or for a massed display, and varieties include those with frilled petals or large, saucer-shaped blooms, in white and tonings of lemon, yellow, gold, orange, rose-pink and orange-pink.

For pot culture the dwarf 'Wonderland' series is ideal, growing to 25 cm (10 in.) with large 10 cm (4 in.) flowers.

PETUNIA HYBRIDA
(PETUNIA)

Suitable for containers, cottage, formal and Mediterranean-style gardens; prefers full sun.

Petunia varieties range from sprawling mounds to erect bushes. They have single, double or frilled flowers in brilliant colours. The 'Multiflora' types have funnel-shaped flowers in a wide colour range. 'Grandifloras' grow 40–60 cm (16–24 in.), and have larger flowers with fringed or frilled edges. 'Dazzler' grows 30–40 cm (12–16 in.), and has smaller flowers and comes in a range of bright colours. Semi-trailing types are available.

Petunia hybrids are useful for mass planting and borders and for pots, tubs, hanging baskets, window boxes or troughs. (The perennial *Petunia* is also suitable for these uses.)

To encourage a second flush of blooms in late summer or early autumn, cut back and fertilise after their first summer flowering.

PHLOX DRUMMONDII
(PHLOX)

Suitable for containers, cottage, formal and Mediterranean-style gardens; prefers full sun.

This hardy, bright, spreading annual flowers in summer. Most varieties have rounded petals with a contrasting white 'eye' in the centre of the flower, others have pointed petals. Phlox is available in a range of colours. Heights vary from tall (45 cm/18 in.) to dwarf compact (20–25 cm/8–10 in.) and extra dwarf (18–20 cm/7–8 in.).

Phlox is ideal for borders and beds, rockeries, containers and window boxes.

PORTULACA GRANDIFLORA
(SUN PLANT)

Suitable for containers and Mediterranean-style gardens; prefers full sun.

Portulaca gives a dazzling display, during the hot summer months, of single or double flowers in white, lemon, lilac, pink, orange, crimson and red. The leaves are grey-green, cylindrical and succulent. The plant has a trailing habit, is 15–20 cm (6–8 in.) tall, and is suitable for raised beds, rockeries, banks, or garden borders.

PRIMULA SPECIES
(FAIRY PRIMROSE)

Suitable for containers, cottage, formal and Mediterranean-style gardens; prefers full or partial shade.

Both annual Primulas, *P. malacoides* and *P. obconica*, perform well in confined spaces.

P. malacoides is a low-growing (15–25 cm/ 6–10 in.), hardy annual, bearing rings of flowers in white, mauve, purple, pink, carmine or ruby. It is ideal for pots, troughs and window boxes in partial sunlight, and looks very attractive if overplanted with bulbs. 'Gilhams White' provides a pleasing contrast when planted with the coloured types. 'Lollipops' is a dwarf mixture for beds or borders.

P. obconica (15–20 cm/6–8 in.) is less tolerant of sun and has larger flowers than *P. malacoides*. Flowers are available in shades of rose, mauve, pale blue, crimson or white. During flowering it may be used as an indoor plant, in a pot or basket, with filtered sunlight.

RUDBECKIA HIRTA
(CONE FLOWER)

Suitable for cottage, formal and Mediterranean-style gardens; prefers full sun.

This tall annual blooms mainly in summer and autumn, and grows 70–90 cm (28–36 in.) The purple to orange-brown daisy-like flowers have dark, raised central cone. Suitable for an accent plant, or bedding or planting in drifts.

SALVIA SPLENDENS
(SCARLET SAGE)

Suitable for containers, cottage, formal and Mediterranean-style gardens; prefers full sun.

The summer flowers are carried on erect spikes. Colours other than scarlet are available, including purple, lavender, pink, orange-pink, cream and white. Most plants grow to 60 cm (2 ft), but it can grow 30–90 cm (1–3 ft).

It provides a colourful bedding or background plant, and is also suitable for window boxes. 'Scarlet Pygmy' is a dwarf

cultivar (to 8 cm/3 in.) and has bright red flowers.

TORENIA FOURNIERI
(WISHBONE FLOWER)

Suitable for containers, cottage and formal gardens; prefers full or partial shade.

This compact (20–30 cm/8–12 in.) summer-flowering annual has showy blooms of deep blue, with yellow and purple markings. A pink cultivar is available. It is suitable for pots or borders.

TROPAEOLUM MAJUS
(NASTURTIUM)

Suitable for containers, cottage and Mediterranean-style gardens; prefers full sun or partial shade.

Nasturtiums will wander, so for small city gardens select from those varieties with compact habits. The dwarf bush hybrids grow to 30 cm (12 in.), and are especially effective in pots or as a uniform edging plant for a path or bed. The 'Jewel' varieties include gold, scarlet, yellow and crimson single flowers. 'Whirlybird' types have semi-double flowers in a wide colour range. 'Alaska' is notable for its cream and green variegated foliage.

VIOLA SPECIES
(PANSY, VIOLA)

Suitable for containers, cottage and formal gardens; prefers partial shade.

V. × wittrockiana (Pansy) and *V. cornuta* (Viola) flower abundantly during spring and summer, grow 15–30 cm (6–12 in.), and are successful in all climatic zones except the very dry. They are sold as seedlings in punnets, or as larger-sized advanced specimens (good for giving the garden an immediate boost).

Both have rich, velvety colours and are very beautiful, but Pansies have a wider variety of colour tones and markings than Violas.

Pansies are useful for pots, window boxes and garden borders. Violas are suitable for pots, window boxes, bedding colour, or for planting over bulbs. Small varieties of Violas, for beds and containers, are 'Johnny Jump Up' and the dwarf 'Bambini'.

ZINNIA ELEGANS
(ZINNIA)

Suitable for containers, cottage, formal and Mediterranean-style gardens; prefers full sun.

These bright and hardy summer-flowering annuals range in heights, flower colours and shapes. For small growers consider 'Lilliput', which grows to 60 cm (24 in.) with small, ball-shaped double flowers in bright and pastel yellow, pink and red; 'Pulcino', which grows to 50 cm (20 in.); or 'Thumbelina', which grows to 20 cm (8 in.) for rockeries, window boxes, pots or edging treatments.

PURCHASING SUPPLIES

Apart from plant nurseries, there is a wide range of outlets selling garden equipment, fertilisers, plants and seeds.

Variety stores generally have a garden section in which you can find pots, watering equipment, metal arches and other garden ornaments, as well as plants and seeds.

Hardware stores also keep some equipment lines, such as watering systems, wheelbarrows, garden tools and equipment.

Produce merchants sell straw and lucerne (excellent for mulching or adding to compost bins), and also bulk fertilisers.

For unusual seeds, plants or bulbs, order from specialty plant clubs. These clubs are often advertised in garden magazines and, if contacted, will be happy to post out catalogues.

Finally, many garden items can be purchased from larger supermarkets, and are easily added to the shopping trolley when doing the regular grocery shopping — a very convenient way to pick up odds and ends for the garden.

Climbing plants add an extra dimension to growing plants in small gardens, but be sure to select a non-rampant type.

Bauhinia corymbosa
(BAUHINIA)

Suitable for containers, cottage and Mediterranean-style gardens; prefers full sun or partial shade.

Bauhinia is an evergreen climber with slender stems and clusters of small, shell-pink orchid-like flowers in spring and autumn. It is delicate in habit and makes a very pretty picture in warmer regions.

Clematis hybrids
(CLEMATIS)

Suitable for containers, cottage, formal and Mediterranean-style gardens; prefers partial shade.

The large flowered *Clematis* hybrids are undoubtedly some of the most beautiful flowering climbers for cool and temperate areas. To give of their best, however, they demand careful management and correct soil and climatic conditions. Ideally, their tops should be in the sun and their roots in the shade.

Gelsemium sempervirens
(CAROLINA YELLOW JASMINE)

Suitable for containers, cottage and formal gardens; prefers full sun or partial shade.

From late winter until mid-spring, this climber provides fragrance and a decorative show of small, yellow, bell-shaped flowers. It has a neat compact habit and pleasant evergreen foliage, making it worthy of wider use.

Hoya carnosa
(WAX PLANT)

Suitable for containers, cottage, formal and Mediterranean-style gardens; prefers partial shade.

A climber of open habit with thick fleshy leaves and umbels of sweetly fragrant pink flowers. It is very decorative trained onto lattice work or a similar support, and is most adaptable to container culture.

Jasminum sambac
(ARABIAN JASMINE)

Suitable for containers, cottage, formal and Mediterranean-style gardens; prefers full sun or partial shade.

Most Jasmines are not suitable for planting in small garden spaces, as they can become invasive and quickly outlive their welcome. *Jasminum sambac* will, however, remain within bounds by being pruned hard after flowering. The small white flowers are heavily perfumed and are enhanced by the glossy deep green foliage. 'Grand Duke of Tuscany' is a double flowered cultivar worthy of a prime position in any garden.

Mandevilla sanderi
(RED BRAZILIAN JASMINE)

Suitable for containers, cottage, formal and Mediterranean-style gardens; prefers partial shade.

Ideal for decorating fences or pergolas or for potting, this evergreen climber supports magnificent pink funnel-form flowers with a yellow throat. It is in bloom for most of the year. Many cultivars are available in different shades of pink.

Solanum jasminoides
(WHITE POTATO VINE)

Suitable for containers, cottage, formal and Mediterranean-style gardens; prefers full sun or partial shade.

Very popular for its clusters of small, papery, white flowers, abundant in summer and early autumn. It is quite trainable for fence or wall coverage as long as some support is provided. It also looks very pretty covering metal or wooden archways.

SOLLYA HETEROPHYLLA
(BLUE-BELL CREEPER)

Suitable for containers, cottage, formal and Mediterranean-style gardens; prefers full sun or partial shade.

A native climber with attractive evergreen foliage and dainty blue bell-shaped flowers in spring and summer, and an effective screening plant much admired by those partial to blue flowers. It is a twining climber, so it will need some support to cover fences or walls.

STEPHANOTIS FLORIBUNDA
(MADASCAR JASMINE)

Suitable for container, cottage, formal and Mediterranean-style gardens; prefers partial shade.

This slender, evergreen climber has large, white, long-lasting, perfumed flowers in summer and early autumn. It requires training over a support and rarely needs to be pruned. *Stephanotis* prefers a sheltered position with its roots in cool soil.

PLANTS FOR SHADY POSITIONS

- *Abutilon* (Chinese Lantern)
- *Agapanthus*
- *Ajuga reptans* (Blue Bugle)
- *Angelica archangelica* (Angelica)
- *Bergenia cordifolia* (Saxifraga)
- *Buxus* species (Box)
- *Camellia* species
- *Campanula medium* (Canterbury Bell)
- *Clematis* hybrids
- *Clethra aborea* (Lily-of-the-Valley Tree)
- *Clivia miniata* (Kaffir Lily)
- *Daphne*
- *Dichondra repans* (Dichondra)
- *Digitalis purpurea* (Foxglove)
- *Elaeocarpus reticulatus* (Blueberry Ash)
- *Fuchsia* hybrids (Fuchsia)
- *Gardenia*
- *Helleborus orientalis* (Lenten Rose)
- *Heterocentron elegans* (Spanish Shawl)
- *Hoya carnosa* (Climbing Wax Plant)
- *Hydrangea macrophylla* (Hydrangea)
- *Mandevilla sanderi* (Red Brazilian Jasmine)
- *Mentha* species (Mint)
- *Primula malacoides* (Fairy Primrose)
- *Primula obconica* (Fairy Primrose)
- *Primula x polyantha* (Polyanthus)
- *Rhododendron* (Azalea)
- *Stephanotis floribunda* (Madagascar Jasmine)
- *Torenia fournieri* (Wishbone Flower)
- *Trachelospermum jasminoides*
- *Vinca minor*
- *Viola cornuta* (Viola)
- *Viola hederacea* (Native Violet)
- *Viola odorata* (Sweet Violet)
- *Viola x wittrockiana* (Pansy)

The following is by no means an exhaustive list of vegetables, but rather a selection of some of the more popular species that can be comfortably accommodated in a small plot.

Your local nursery will also be able to advise you on small and miniature vegetables suitable for containers and small gardens. Specialist seed suppliers, seed clubs and seed networks are other sources of unusual varieties.

BEANS

French beans, as distinct from broad beans, are warm-season, frost-susceptible plants. They are an easy crop to grow, requiring little attention other than regular watering and good drainage. Mulching will prevent moisture loss and keep the roots cool. Select a sheltered position in the garden to avoid wind damage. Beans are susceptible to wet feet, cold snaps and extreme heat, which can all reduce pod setting. The growing period is 10–12 weeks from planting to harvesting.

To save space, climbing beans can be planted over lattice or climbing frames; they take longer to yield than dwarf beans, but they provide for easier harvesting, will produce a heavier crop, and will continue bearing for several weeks.

BEETROOT

This is one of the easiest vegetables to grow, and is particularly delicious when picked young and used small. Although a cool-season crop, there are beetroot varieties that will prosper in all but extreme climatic zones. Well-drained soil is required and only moderate fertilising to prevent forking. Sow seed direct, as transplants are not always successful. Beetroots are at their peak when just short of maturity.

Start pulling alternate roots early, 8 to 10 weeks from sowing seeds, thereby spreading the harvest and allowing extra space for the remaining roots.

BROAD BEANS

These winter vegetables are best suited to mild-temperate and cold climates. Sow seed direct in autumn and early winter. Maturing 18–20 weeks after sowing, they are ready to be harvested in late winter and early spring.

A well-limed, sharply drained soil with reasonable fertility is preferred, along with a sunny aspect and ample water during the growing season. A high level of phosphorus is desirable. Too much nitrogen is detrimental, promoting excessive leaf growth at the expense of flowers and pods. Harvest immature pods for best flavour — older pods harden and become floury. Regular picking encourages further pod setting.

BROCCOLI

This is a cool-season vegetable. Sow seed or plant seedlings in summer. Harvest 16 weeks from seed, or 12 weeks from transplanting seedlings.

Broccoli is tolerant of light or heavy soil as long as sufficient fertiliser has been used. Plants checked in growth will be of inferior quality. Side dressing with a highly nitrogenous fertiliser, and providing ample and regular water, will maintain satisfactory growth. Best results are obtained by planting a broccoli crop in soil that has previously grown legumes.

BRUSSELS SPROUTS

These biennial plants require a cold period to flower, and are best restricted to cool climates. They are a useful vegetable for the autumn and winter growing period. Sow seed or plant seedlings in early summer in cold districts, and allow 16–20 weeks to grow to maturity.

Sprouts are tolerant of a wide range of soils and treatments, but to obtain sweet, delicately flavoured buds, the plants should not be checked by dryness or too much heat. Apply a dressing of complete fertiliser at bed-preparation stage, supported by side dressings to boost the crop during growth.

CABBAGE

Of the brassicas (cabbage, cauliflower, broccoli), cabbage is the most tolerant of and adaptable to climate variations. It can be grown over a wide range of temperatures, providing it is started in the warm weather to mature in the cooler months (otherwise it will run to seed, causing the head to lose its food value). Grow cabbages quickly to form tight, solid heads.

They prefer a sunny position in a light, moderately fertile, open loan, enriched with rotted animal manure or garden compost. Efficient drainage is essential; however, during active growth and especially in dry weather, the plants require copious quantities of water supplied at regular intervals. Mulch to prevent excessive moisture loss and keep roots cool. Cabbages are gross feeders and respond vigorously to fertilising.

The smaller roundhead and sugarloaf cabbages are suited to small-scale vegetable plots.

A mini cabbage that matures earlier than regular cabbage, and can be spaced at 30 cm (1 ft) intervals to produce a head of 1 kg (2 lb), is available through specialist seed networks.

CAPSICUM

This is a warm-season crop, and in warm regions can be grown year round. Prepare the bed initially with complete fertiliser and side dress during growth. Harvest 12 weeks from transplanting seedlings.

Capsicums can be picked at any stage of development; however, leaving the fruit of the 'Giant Sweet Bell' varieties to mature on the plant will result in a sweeter flavour and the development of striking yellow, orange and red colours.

Capsicums are particularly ornamental plants and make attractive tub subjects for the patio, courtyard or sunny terrace. As in-ground plants they are ideal for small plots, as they bear heavily. One or two plants in the garden is sufficient for the average family.

CARROTS

These are favourite home-grown vegetables. Although cool-season vegetables, they are tolerant of various climates and it is possible to crop carrots successively through spring, summer and autumn.

Provide them with a sunny position and a light soil with an open structure. Sow seed direct and successively through spring, summer and autumn.

Apply a light nitrogenous foliar spray during growth, but do not plant into soil fertilised with fresh animal manure or the roots may become deformed. Water should be evenly applied, as alternating wet and dry soil can lead to cracking of the root.

Most varieties require 16–20 weeks to mature, whilst the smaller 'baby' varieties may be ready in 10–12 weeks.

Miniature varieties are available to growers with limited space, shallow soil or those confined to pot culture. These are gaining popularity for both their ease of culture and their culinary qualities.

CAULIFLOWER

Cauliflower is a cool-season vegetable and is demanding in its climatic requirements. It is difficult to grow in warm regions because a cold temperature is necessary to initiate curd development.

Cauliflowers thrive in a sunny position in a deeply dug, well-manured loam. Sow seed or plant seedlings in warm ground from early summer to early autumn. Good drainage is essential combined with a generous soaking of water once a week. A number of different varieties are available within three groups — early, mid and late season — making it possible to harvest cauliflowers over an extended period of 10 to 12 weeks.

Mini cauliflowers are easy to grow, and can be spaced at close intervals to produce a crop of small 10 cm (4 in.) curds. They mature 4 months from sowing.

CELERY

This is a hungry, lime-loving vegetable that thrives in a climate with a long season of warm days and cool nights with medium to low humidity. It must be grown quickly to produce top-quality stalks. Rich, moist, well-drained soil in a sunny position is ideal. Sow seed or plant seedlings in spring and summer. Regular watering and foliar feeds are recommended. Harvest in 3 to 4 months from transplanting, when the stems reach 15–20 cm (6–8 in.).

CORN

Corn is a tall crop and occupies a good deal of garden space, and should therefore only be considered if the kitchen garden is large enough to support it.

Corn should be grown in blocks rather than rows, as it is pollinated by wind, and this ensures maximum fertilisation; a 25–30 cm (10–12 in.) grid pattern is ideal.

Sow seed direct in spring and summer in beds that have been well prepared with applications of organic matter and complete fertiliser with a high nitrogen content. Liberal amounts of water are also required to grow corn successfully. Harvest in 12 to 16 weeks after sowing.

If the desire to grow a corn crop is strong, but space is very limited, mini varieties that have smaller cobs or shorter stalks are worth seeking out.

CUCUMBER

Sow seed or plant seedlings in spring in soil that is well-drained, reasonably fertile, and prepared with organic matter or fertiliser. Cucumber is a frost-sensitive plant, so avoid setting out too early in spring in frosty areas. As cucumber vines are rampant spreaders, the city gardener will have difficulty providing sufficient space for a crop unless trellises are used to create vertical growing areas, or a compact hybrid (suitable for large pots or tubs) is chosen.

EGGPLANT

Eggplant (also known as aubergine) grows in summer and requires warm conditions over a 5 month period to achieve quality fruit. Deep, free-draining sandy soils are preferable. Add compost and generous amounts of animal manure when preparing the bed. Sow seed direct or purchase seedlings. Expect to harvest crops 16 weeks from setting plants out.

For the small eggplant varieties used in Thai cooking, consult the catalogues of specialty seed companies and heritage seed suppliers and clubs.

GARLIC

Garlic is propagated by cloves, planted in spring at a depth of 8 cm (3 in.), spaced 15 cm (6 in.) apart. Use only well-developed bulbs for propagation purposes. Provide a rich fertile loam, occasional side dressings or nitrogenous fertiliser, and ample water during the growth period; the plant is otherwise undemanding in culture. Harvest 8 months after germination.

LETTUCE

Lettuce can be grown in a wide range of moderately rich, well-drained soils. It is a gross feeder; when provided with well-rotted manure or a high-nitrogen, liquid fertiliser, it thrives. As lettuce has poorly developed roots to support its massive leaf structure, it is important to maintain adequate moisture levels. Water efficiently by applying in the cool of the evening. There is a wide variety of compact lettuces suited to the small-scale potager. These adapt well to pot culture as long as they are regularly watered. All small lettuces are ready to harvest 60–75 days from transplanting. Successive sowings of 5–10 seeds every fortnight through spring, summer and autumn will provide continual harvests.

'Mignonette' is useful for hotter districts. Other excellent varieties are 'Cos' (long leaves), and 'Buttercrunch' (small, thick, waxy leaves), 'Red Oakleaf' and 'Lollo Rosso' (Coral Lettuce).

ONIONS AND SHALLOTS

These members of the *Allium* family need a light, well-drained medium to heavy loam with added organic matter in a sunny position. They do not tolerate acidity, so liming may be necessary. Onions may be sown from seed or grown from seedlings; shallots may be planted from division of a clump. Onions generally take 6–8 months to develop; in smaller kitchen gardens it is sometimes not practical to devote a bed to one crop for that period of time. Shallots, which mature in 8 to 12 weeks, can be planted as an alternative.

PEAS

Peas are sparse croppers so, before planting, carefully consider their value relative to ground space occupied. The edible-podded peas, such as snow peas and sugar snap peas, are a better choice for the tiny kitchen garden. They perform well under cool, moist conditions. They are sensitive to heat; temperatures above 30°C (85°F) will reduce yields. Frost will also affect flowering and subsequent cropping.

POTATOES

Potatoes can be grown in a small kitchen garden; one plant will yield a nest of lovely tubers if the soil is rich. However, it would be impossible even in a large kitchen garden to produce all the potatoes required for household consumption. Buy certified seed potatoes to avoid disease problems; nurseries stock packs of different varieties along with directions on growing and cooking.

'Sebago' (oval shape, smooth, white skin, shallow eyes) is a popular cultivar and a good all-rounder. 'Pontiac' (round, thin red skin, white flesh, deep eyes) is delicious cooked in the jacket, baked or mashed. For chips, choose 'Russet Burbank' or 'Kennebec' (white skin, white flesh). 'Bintje' (cream skin, yellow flesh, excellent flavour and texture) is useful for potato salad. 'Patrione' (cream skin, yellow flesh) also suits this purpose and is a suitable

addition to casseroles, but does not mash smoothly. 'Desiree', a Dutch variety (oval, pink skin, cream flesh, delicately textured), is ideal for baking, roasting and mashing. 'Toolangi Delight' (purplish skin, white flesh, dry textured) is useful for mashing, boiling and baking.

PUMPKIN

Pumpkin prefers a warm, sunny spot with protection from strong winds and can be grown in all climatic zones, except the very coldest. Be generous with organic matter and water; ensure soil is well drained. As the vines are rambling and have large leaves, city dwellers planning on cultivating them should focus on the smaller bush varieties that are available, some of which can even be grown in tubs. Vines can also be trellised to save space.

'Baby Blue' (spherical shape, grey-blue skin, pale orange flesh) has a compact vine, good storage life, and is early maturing (in 14 weeks). 'Blue Max' gives a heavy yield of fruit. 'Butterbush' is ideal for a small garden or large tub, and 'Butternut' (pear shape, beige skin, orange flesh) is a hearty cropper. 'Cinderella' and 'Golden Nugget' take up little room in a small plot; the latter producing about 6 small, orange-red fruit on each plant.

RADISH

Radish crops are easily cultivated and take up very little space. Radishes come in different shapes and sizes, and may be divided into two groups: quick-growing small types and large winter radishes. The early maturing cultivars with small, round roots are ideal for growing in limited space or in containers.

Grow radishes quickly, to achieve optimum flavour and texture. A rich soil with added organic matter and a pre-planting fertiliser plus ample water during the growing period will promote rapid growth. Liquid feeds can be given fortnightly. Harvest the crop 4–6 weeks from sowing seed.

RHUBARB

Rhubarb is a useful vegetable to cultivate in a kitchen garden, as it is delicious stewed and added to pies, but it requires permanent space for 4 or 5 years of cropping, so only consider it if the space available warrants this. Soil preparation is vital. It is a gross feeder, so incorporate organic matter, compost and complete fertiliser before planting. It resents waterlogging; a raised bed is ideal. When harvesting, remember that the crowns may be set back by careless picking: snap off the stems from the outside inwards. Harvest all thin stems so that the plants can channel energy into producing thicker, longer ones.

SILVERBEET

It is adaptable to cool and warm climates, and is one of the handiest pick-and-come-again leaf vegetables. Sow seed or plant seedlings in spring and summer in most districts. In warm zones winter sowing is also viable. Fertilise with a nitrogenous plant food plus blood and bone or poultry manure side dressings. Harvest 8 to 12 weeks from seed sowing.

TOMATOES

These are one of the most popular home grown vegetables; an excellent crop for the kitchen garden, as the plants produce a high yield relative to the space occupied, and the fruit can be harvested over a 2-month period. All tomatoes are relatively demanding subjects, requiring vigilant watering, pruning and fertilising practices in order to produce good yields. Sow seeds or plant seedlings in warm spring soil. A base dressing of complete fertiliser or heavy manuring is needed. Foliar spray at frequent intervals when fruit begins to set. Harvest is possible 12–14 weeks after transplanting.

For those in minute gardens, there is an extensive range of mini varieties, with cherry-sized fruit, which are ideal for pots, window boxes or planters. Some are available in seed packs from general nursery outlets, while others need to be ordered from seed clubs or seedsavers networks.

Some of the larger fruited varieties can be suitably accommodated in the small kitchen garden, by staking and careful pruning. Some tomato plants can be left as bushes or pruned and staked — the latter method produces fewer fruits but of much better quality and weight.

ZUCCHINI, MARROW AND SUMMER SQUASH

These cucurbits are prized for their delicious fruits and edible flowers. Incorporate manure or compost during bed preparation. Add complete fertiliser prior to sowing or transplanting. Sow in spring, applying regular water. Harvest within 7 to 8 weeks. When picked frequently, cropping will be boosted and heavy yields attained. These cucurbits are space hogs; there are, however, smaller types suited to small-scale gardening.

The following is by no means an exhaustive list of fruits and berries, but rather a selection of some of the more popular types that can be comfortably accommodated in a small plot and will provide optimum value from each plant.

CITRUS TREES

Citrus trees can be grown in the garden or in tubs. Their glossy leaves provide interest even when their flowers and fruit are absent, and they look very pretty when underplanted with annuals. Cumquats are ideal for tubs, and mandarins and 'Valencia' oranges are all easily kept to attractive shapes.

Tubs of citrus trees are ideal for a Mediterranean-style garden. Mandarin and cumquat trees lend themselves to clipping as standards, and would suit the formal garden.

For a good citrus crop, water regularly and feed two or three times a year with a general fertiliser.

STRAWBERRIES

Strawberries are easy to grow, do not require much space and, having many cultivars, bear in a continuing sequence. To grow strawberries well, situate them in a sunny position. Prepare the soil with compost, animal manure and a complete fertiliser prior to planting. Planting in barrels and tubs is effective; raised beds ensure good drainage and ease of picking.

Nurseries stock varieties suited to local areas, but always check whether they are certified virus free. The little alpine strawberry is delicious, and well worth growing in the smaller kitchen garden, as it is a bushy form and does not produce runners. Propagation is by seed.

KIWI FRUIT AND PASSIONFRUIT

These vines will cover a pergola, and will provide shade, shelter and seclusion whilst being productive. Growing them on a pergola also enables the fruit to be easily harvested. Kiwi fruit grows on a twining, deciduous vine. It thrives in mild climates where there are no spring frosts. It requires adequate moisture as the shallow root system must not be allowed to dry out. Add organic matter and some liquid fertiliser, as it is a heavy feeder.

Passionfruit is a popular vine fruit: the flowers are attractive, and it makes excellent coverage for a pergola or trellis in a sunny position. Good rich soil with plenty of plant food and sharp drainage are essential. Frost protection may be required in the first season, thereafter they are quite hardy. Suitable for cooler areas is the banana passionfruit, which has long, yellow, more acid fruit. It is a vigorous and productive plant that grows well without too much attention.

MELONS

Watermelon, rockmelon and honeydew are relatives of the pumpkin and as such have similar, large-leafed, wandering vines. Careful selection of small and midget varieties means that these fruits can be grown even in the smallest of kitchen gardens.

The following list includes many of the mainstay culinary herbs; it is by no means exhaustive, and many other interesting herbs are obtainable which may not be of use in the kitchen but are desirable for their ornamental value (that is, texture, habit or aroma) or for their medicinal or companion-planting properties.

ALLIUM SATIVUM
(GARLIC)

Garlic is a member of the onion family. It is a perennial, and grows 60–90 cm (2–3 ft). Dig up the bulbs when the leaves wither.

To propagate, divide the bulb. Garlic likes a rich, moist (not wet), sandy loam and a sunny position. It will resist frost but not drought.

ALLIUM SCHOENOPRASUM
(CHIVES)

Chives are small members of the onion family. Perennial in habit, chives develop into thick, leafy clumps, making great fillers in a herb garden or pot. They grow to 60 cm (2 ft) in height. As chives are so attractive, with their linear leaves and rosy mauve flowers, they are often used as small edging plants in the flower garden.

Propagate by sowing seed or dividing clumps. Partial shade is tolerated but good drainage is essential. Liquid feed to boost leaf production from spring to autumn.

ANETHUM GRAVEOLENS
(DILL)

Dill is an annual and grows 60–120 cm (2–4 ft) high. The leaves are blue-green and the flowers are small and yellow.

Dill can be raised from seed sown direct into the bed. Full sun, well-prepared soil with added organic matter and good drainage are needed to support optimum growth. Protect plants from the wind.

ANGELICA ARCHANGELICA
(ANGELICA)

Angelica is a biennial with large leaves, hollow stems and clusters of pale green flowers in the second season.

Growing to 2 m (7 ft), it is a very useful background plant. Greenish white clusters of flowers appear in spring and autumn.

Angelica can be grown from seed or from root cuttings. It resists drought and frost, but requires a moist, rich soil in the semi-shade. It needs wind protection, as the stems are brittle.

ARTEMISIA SPECIES
(TARRAGON)

Tarragon is perennial and dies back in winter. It can grow 60–150 cm (2–5 ft) in height.

Artemisia dracunculus (French Tarragon) is the preferred tarragon for culinary purposes, as *A. dracunculoides* (Russian, or False Tarragon) has less flavour.

Tarragon is grown from divisions of established plants. It is drought and frost resistant, but full sun and well-drained soil with added organic matter are necessary.

Old plants tend to become woody, and should be lifted and divided every second or third year in spring or autumn.

BORAGO OFFICINALIS
(BORAGE)

Borage has thick, branching stems, large, grey-green, hairy leaves, and sky blue star-shaped flowers. It grows 30–90 cm (1–3 ft) high.

Borage is propagated by seed. Native to the Mediterranean region, it thrives in full sun on any reasonable soil. It is undemanding in its requirements and is a good choice for novice herb gardeners.

CORIANDRUM SATIVUM
(CORIANDER)

Coriander is a hardy annual, with bright green leaves and white, mauve or pink flowers. It can grow to 60 cm (2 ft) high.

Coriander can be propagated from seed sown year round in moderate climates; spring in cold areas. Full sun suits it best, but plants should be shaded from the afternoon sun in hot summer areas.

FOENICULUM VULGARE
(FENNEL)

A mature height of 1.5 m (5 ft) makes this perennial an excellent background border plant or focal point in the herb garden. Umbrels of bright yellow flowers appear in summer and early autumn.

Fennel will self-sow, but can be propagated by sowing a few seeds direct in clumps in late spring; thin to the strongest seedling. It adapts to most well-drained soils and will resist frost and drought. It likes a sunny position and needs wind protection.

LEVISTICUM OFFICINALE
(LOVAGE)

Lovage is a strikingly ornamental herb; the dark green glossy leaves and umbels of small yellow flowers ensure it has a prime position in the herb garden. It is a perennial plant, and will grow to a height of 2 m (7 ft).

It will adapt to most soils and positions, but is not suited to hot areas. Sow seed in late summer in a full sun or partial shade position.

MENTHA SPECIES
(MINT)

Mint has various forms, including: *Mentha spicata* (Common Mint), *M. viridis* (Spearmint), *M. piperita* (Peppermint), *M. suaveolens* (Applemint), *M. suaveolens* 'Variegata' (Pineapple mint) and *M. pulegium* (Pennyroyal).

All mints propagate by runners and are invasive, so should be grown in enclosed beds or pots. Potted plants can be sunk into the ground, to contain the root system.

Mints are hardy perennials, and will root readily. Choose a warm, sunny aspect and water regularly.

OCIMUM BASILICUM
(SWEET OR COMMON BASIL)

Basil is an annual plant. It grows 50–75 cm (20–30 in.) high and is suitable for containers.

Propagate from seed sown in spring, and tip prune to encourage bushiness.

Select a sunny position, or a warm and semi-shaded position in hot and tropical areas. Basil will resist frost but dislikes the cold. The soil should be kept damp but not wet.

ORIGANUM MAJORANA
(MARJORAM)

Marjoram is suited to pots and hanging baskets, and grows 30–60 cm (1–2 ft) high. It is a perennial, but is sometimes grown as an annual because it may die out in cold, wet winters. It is necessary to replace plants every 3 or 4 years, in any event.

Propagate by seeds, cuttings or root division. Plant in full sun, and do not allow the soil to dry out. Marjoram will not tolerate drought or frost.

ORIGANUM VULGARE
(OREGANO, OR WILD MARJORAM)

Oregano is a perennial with a mat-like, creeping habit and grows to 75 cm (2½ ft) in height. It features dark green leaves and small clusters of purple summer flowers, and makes an effective groundcover.

Propagate from seed or by division of old plants. It likes a sunny position, and will tolerate frost but not drought.

PETROSELINUM SPECIES
(PARSLEY)

Petroselinum crispum (Curled Parsley) and *P. neopolitanum* (Italian Parsley) are suitable for growing in large pots or tubs, and all types pf parsley are effective used as low hedges in the herb garden or vegetable plot.

When harvesting, pick leaves from the outside of the plant, as new growth takes place from the centre of the crown.

Parsley is grown from seed sown in spring. A moist well-drained, moderately rich soil gives best results.

ROSMARINUS SPECIES
(ROSEMARY)

Rosemary can be used as an ornamental feature in the herb garden, used as a low hedge, or trained against walls or fences. It has very fragrant, narrow, dark green, leathery leaves. Its flowers are small, pale blue or white, and appear in spring and summer.

It can be raised from seeds or cuttings. Plant in full sun on a well-drained, quite poor, dry soil. Pinch pruning will encourage bushiness. Rosemary will resist drought and frost, and tolerates coastal conditions.

SALVIA OFFICINALIS
(SAGE)

This evergreen herb is an excellent plant for growing in containers. It will grow 50–60 cm (20–24 in.) in height.

Full sun and rather dryish soil is preferred; a raised bed will ensure good drainage. Propagate from seed sown in spring or autumn or by cuttings taken in early summer. Sage will resist drought and frost.

THYMUS SPECIES
(THYME)

Thyme varieties are all neat little plants and, according to their habit, can be used for groundcover, dwarf edgings and small specimen plants.

Propagate by seed, cuttings or root division. Sunny, protected positions are preferred and, although sharp drainage is essential, apply moderate amounts of water in hot dry weather.

TROPAEOLUM MAJUS
(NASTURTIUM)

Nasturtium is a perennial, but is frequently treated as an annual, particularly in cooler areas. There are many dwarf varieties suitable for small spaces. The leaves of the 'Alaska' hybrid are so pretty with their splashes of white that this compact plant can be grown for the foliage alone. It makes a stylish edging plant, or can be potted and allowed to spill over urns as a focal point of the herb garden.

Nasturtium prefers full sun, but will tolerate part shade. Sow seed to raise plants. If grown for flowers and fruit, a well-drained, dryish, sandy soil is ideal; if grown for leaves, plant in an organically enriched soil.

Index

References to page numbers with a B indicate boxed material; P indicates a photograph; D indicates a drawing; T indicates a table; page numbers in **bold** indicate a main reference.